AIKIDO
"CENTEREDNESS"

A NEW CLASS TO DEVELOP
POWERS OF THE CENTER
ENHANCING ALL ASPECTS
OF DAILY LIFE

PRESENTED BY
BOULDER AIKIKAI

instructor:
HIROSHI IKEDA 7TH DAN

assistant instructors:
JUDE BLITZ 3RD DAN Certified Hakomi Therapist
SUE ROBINSON 2ND DAN Artist
RON MEYER 1ST DAN Video Producer

EVERY TUESDAY, WEDNESDAY & THURSDAY EVENING
6:00PM - 7:00PM

CROSSROADS GARDEN, 1800 30TH STREET, SUITE 206, BOULDER
(EAST OF CROSSROADS MALL, BETWEEN ARAPAHOE & WALNUT)

$60 PER MONTH OR $100 FOR TWO MONTHS

THIS CLASS IS DESIGNED FOR THOSE WHO WISH TO EXPLORE CENTER
WITHOUT ENGAGING IN THE FULL MARTIAL ARTS ASPECT OF AIKIDO.

ADULTS OF ALL AGES WELCOME (above 16 years, please)
WEAR LOOSE AND COMFORTABLE CLOTHING
PRE-REGISTRATION NOT REQUIRED

FOR MORE INFORMATION PLEASE CALL 444-5013

CENTER
The Power of Aikido

Ron Meyer and Mark Reeder

BASED ON STUDIES WITH HIROSHI IKEDA SENSEI

FROG, LTD.
BERKELEY, CALIFORNIA

Center: The Power of Aikido

Published by
Frog, Ltd.
Frog, Ltd. books are distributed by North Atlantic Books,
P.O. Box 12327, Berkeley, California 94712
Cover and book design by Nancy Koerner
Printed in the United States of America

Library of Congress Cataloging-in-Publication Data
Meyer, Ron, 1943–
Center : the power of aikido, from the teachings of Hiroshi Ikeda / by Ron Meyer and Mark Reeder.
    p.   cm.
ISBN 1-58394-012-x
1. Aikido. I. Title: Power of aikido. II. Meyer, Ron, 1943– III. Reeder, Mark. IV. Title.

GV1114.35 .I54 1999
    796.815'4--dc21   99-050135

1 2 3 4 5 6 7 8 9 / 04 03 02 01 00

CONTENTS

PREFACE

All the exchanges incorporated into this book are amalgams of numerous questions and answers gleaned from our forty years of combined experience in the martial arts. In addition, the Socratic structure of the text is completely our responsibility and is a didactic convention used to present the centering principles and Second Level Training techniques in a logical format. We selected the interrogative method of inquiry—using ourselves to ask and answer the questions—because the martial arts are more a collection of insights, aphorisms, and stories than a coherent body of knowledge amenable to systemization. In addition, the Socratic approach has a long history of use for explaining martial arts principles. Even so, it is our opinion that the best way for the reader to learn and understand these concepts is to explore their validity in actual training and fighting situations.

INTRODUCTION BY THE AUTHORS

The American Aikido experience has thrived for more than forty years, since Koichi Tohei Sensei first brought the art to Hawaii in 1957. From that island paradise Aikido emigrated to the West Coast of the United States, staking footholds in Los Angeles and San Francisco. In the early sixties, it leap-frogged over the vast midsection of the continent to the eastern shore, where it took root in New York and Boston. From both coasts, it spread inland, until by the end of the century nearly every major metropolitan area and most mid-sized communities boasted Aikido dojo.

Aikido had its origins in the first half of the 20th century with Morihei Ueshiba, known in Aikido tradition as "O Sensei"—the great teacher. As a boy in the late 1800's, he had watched his father beaten by gang members and vowed to make himself strong. O Sensei's training in the martial arts was severe and he often pushed his body past its physical limits. In order to strengthen his skull, for instance, he beat his head against a stone pillar, earning himself the sobriquet "stonehead." He also trained furiously for days in the mountains.

As a result, he eventually attained the status of an undefeated fighter with an enlightened spirit, on a par with the renowned Japanese sword master Miyamoto Musashi. Terry Dobson, one of O Sensei's few non-Japanese *uchi deshi*, or personal students, described Aikido's founder as a superlative martial artist who, "functioned on another plane" and was "a quantum leap above others."

O Sensei was still alive when Aikido came to the U.S., where his unflagging spirit and dedication to intense training evoked great excitement in American practioners. In those early days of Aikido in America, the emphasis was on hard physical training and there were few discussions about *ki* or self realization. O Sensei's precept of *agatsu*—victory over oneself—was widely interpreted as an admonition to push beyond one's physical limits. Americans were quick to emulate the harsh training O Sensei required from his *uchi deshi* and workouts were severe and often brutal. Francis Takahashi Sensei recalled a typical Saturday workout in Los Angeles: "We would wake up early, then train for four hours. Afterward, we would go for a five mile run on the beach, return to the dojo and train for four more hours. Then in the late afternoon we would go out for another run."

When O Sensei died in 1969, two developments occurred. Koichi Tohei Sensei became the chief instructor at Hombu, Aikido's world headquarters in Tokyo. He was also the best-known Aikido representative in the west and many dojo in California thought of him as their primary teacher. Tohei Sensei realized that the tradition of brutal training wasn't the only way to teach Aikido and he began to espouse the concept of *ki* and the energy body.

Secondly, many Americans who had spent several years training abroad in Japan either directly under Aikido's founder or with his most highly ranked students, returned home with their own unique grasp of the art. Among them were Robert Nadeau, Mary Heiny, and Terry Dobson. Impressed by the seemingly magical demonstrations of Aikido skill that they had witnessed in Japan, they began teaching U.S. audiences that the spiritual and physical accomplishments of O Sensei were within everyone's grasp.

For fifteen years these and other American pioneers proselytized their views of Aikido throughout the United States. As before, the greatest growth remained in California. While translating Aikido into a powerful metaphor for such activities as conflict resolution and personal growth, few Aikido students were actually transformed spiritually and none were able to duplicate O Sensei's powerful techniques.

In the late 1980's, as Ron Meyer and John Stone began conducting interviews for their book, *Aikido in America*, many senior American Sensei became disenchanted with the emphasis on rote repetition of techniques, hard training, and spiritual visualizations that had so far not produced any cosmic revelations or invincible martial artists. These teachers and practioners then began asking what was wrong, putting forth and exploring many ideas.

Ron Meyer focused on two fundamental principles: a defender's ability to receive a blow without debilitating results; and the process preceding the execution of a technique that made the technique effortless and effective.

The ability to receive a blow without being incapacitated by it appears to be an oxymoron. In the famous Ali-Frazier fight—the "Thrilla in Manila"—both fighters, though badly damaged from the terrific blows they received, were still standing at the end of the bout. Terry Dobson adamantly maintained during his interviews for *Aikido in America* that O Sensei had told him: "When a strike comes, you cannot collapse with it, you cannot fight with it, you must receive it."

The capacity to throw an opponent effortlessly also seems contradictory. Olympic-caliber wrestling is a case in a point: wrestlers train daily for hours at a time to prepare for a three-minute match that leaves them drained at the end. Any thoughts of effortless throws are considered fantasies. Yet Dan Gable, the celebrated U.S. wrestler who won a gold medal at the Munich Games in 1972, did so with a strained knee. Physically unable to overpower many of his opponents, he won by wrestling at a plane above his competitors.

Over a decade later, Aikido teacher and conflict management expert Tom Crum has observed, "If I just try to take someone down or throw them, I'll have lots of problems. They will adjust. First, I have to disturb their balance. In this state the throw comes from a secondary movement or pressure, i.e., from the center. Disturbing a person's balance is different than moving them off their spot."

The possibility of receiving powerful attacks and then throwing an opponent with little or no effort intrigued both of us greatly. Then, in the summer of 1993, Boulder Aikikai's chief instructor, Hiroshi Ikeda Sensei, began a class outside of the regular dojo, called simply the "Centering Class." For those of us who participated in the Centering Class, it was clear that Sensei was working on something that for us was exciting and new to our experience of Aikido. It was also, at times, unfathomable.

Bereft of the sounds of exertion that usually accompanied Ikeda's vigorous and distinctive style of training, at first it seemed that little was being achieved. However, as the months passed, those who remained witnessed the exploration of manipulating power in the martial arts. These classes laid out the means for effectively and unequivocally reducing an attacker's power so that an Aikido technique could be applied.

When the Centering Class moved to the regular dojo a year-and-a-half later, Ikeda Sensei asked Ron to continue teaching the centering class, which he did until the spring of 1999. Meanwhile, Mark began introducing these ideas to students in his beginners classes.

In 1997 we discussed the possibility of systematizing what by then we had defined as "centering principles" and compiling them into a book. Over the next year we came up with a conceptual structure that we call Second Level Training (SLT).

SLT looks beyond the basic movement and technique training inherent in all martial arts and examines the underlying factors of power and how we incorporate it into our movement. In addition, SLT develops applications of power that can be used to neutralize the speed, strength, and size of an opponent.

One of the more troublesome aspects of writing this book was choosing terminology to define the concept of SLT. To begin with, the term "Second Level Training" implies that it is the next step after basic movement training. However, that terminology may reflect our own experience rather than a fundamental learning sequence. In fact, we believe that the concepts described in this book can be learned from the very beginning of martial arts training. Secondly, terms such as "centeredness," "uprooting," and "grounding," for example, share commonalities with other martial arts. We have therefore attempted to explain SLT in a manner applicable to novices and familiar to other martial arts practioners.

We offer the observation from our own experience that the concepts and training discussed here, and the process for learning them, requires time, focus, and diligence. Initially, we spent much time unlearning certain ideas regarding movement that simply did not work in real-world situations. Then, we had to retrain our minds to overcome the human tendency to persist stubbornly at an ineffective technique or movement simply because its pattern was ingrained in our muscle memory. As a result, the purpose of the book is to direct the reader to techniques that expedite the process of learning.

In the creation of *Center: the Power of Aikido*, we are deeply indebted to George Leonard and John Stone for their editorial insights in the initial draft of the manuscript. Among the many other people unconnected with Boulder Aikikai who assisted us, Mike Sigman and Wendy Palmer were very kind with their criticisms in the book's early incarnations, while Justin Lowe, our editor for North Atlantic Books, made us sound more readable than we really are. Further, we would like to acknowledge the students at Boulder Aikikai who wittingly and unwittingly helped us as we pursued the theories set forth in this book during nightly classes—especially the twenty or so regular members of Ron Meyer's Friday night Centering Class. These students provided him with the opportunity to apply this book's ideas to see how they worked. Ron is especially thankful for the continued support of Doug Smith.

We would also like to thank, Debbie Kranzler, Manson Root, Tracy Alpert and Bill Sackett for their help in preparing the manuscript. Our families put up with endless conversations about concepts in the book, early-morning phone calls, and other disruptions as some piece of information would enthrall us at the expense of our personal lives. We thank them for their understanding, patience, and thesaurus skills.

Finally, with much love and respect, we would like to thank our teacher, Hiroshi Ikeda, Sensei of Boulder Aikikai, for giving us the chance to be present as he taught and practiced Aikido.

PHOTO CREDITS

The authors would like to thank Rick Santos, Julie Poitras-Santos, Debbie Kranzler and John Locatelli for being the models for the photographs in this book. We would also like to thank Diane Evans for the descriptive photographs.

THE PHILOSOPHY BEHIND SECOND LEVEL TRAINING

To comprehend the philosophy behind Second Level Training, (SLT) students have to break with conventional Aikido wisdom in four important ways. First, stressing mindless physical training and repetition is not sufficient to achieve advanced levels of expertise. Second, Aikido has not been laid down once and for all by O Sensei. Third, the traditional master-student relationship is antiquated. Fourth, immersion in Japanese culture is not necessary to understand Aikido.

1) At first glance, SLT appears contradictory. According to many teachers, all martial arts come from movement. Yet these same instructors are also fond of pointing out that ninety percent of improvement in the martial arts is mental. We believe what they are saying is that philosophizing without training, and hard training without questioning, analyzing, and studying will greatly retard your progress and perhaps bring you to a point of stagnation in your martial arts development.

If you swing the bokken one thousand times a day, you will likely become an expert at swinging the bokken. However, mere repetition of a physical practice does not mean that you will improve your martial understanding. You have to ask questions regarding why you are swinging the bokken. Conversely, if you think only about the bokken and its function as a weapon, you'll never have a physical understanding of the bokken or of the connection between bokken and body.

2) One way to view Aikido is as an eternally determined system of training, that is immutable, and to consider that O Sensei merely discovered it. This point of view depicts Do, *or The Way, as a path literally laid down for all time. Those who travel that path, if they travel far enough, will find the unknown. If this premise is correct, then Aikido is not finished and never will be. Another way to think of this is to ask yourself, "if O Sensei were alive today, don't you think that Aikido would still be growing and evolving? "*

3) Today, the martial arts, and Aikido in particular, have a previously unrealized opportunity to diversify, because they no longer have to remain within the confines of one martial style or another. Secrecy regarding fighting techniques and an alliance to one master is no longer necessary, and should not continue to be such a strong focus of the martial arts. More important is the study of movement in relation to the body, ground, and attacking force. Martial artists can now be more open and honest about their "powers." Early Japanese teachers often kept secrets from their students, greatly inhibiting their growth. If someone had told us about SLT from the beginning, our Aikido would be very different today.

4) Most of us have noticed that "how we view reality" has a direct impact on our experience and effectiveness in the world. The story is told that the natives of Tierra del Fuego could not see Darwin's ship, The Beagle, because the way in which they viewed the world did not allow for a ship so big. It is the same in martial arts: one person facing an attacker's strong punch is excited by the possibility of dealing with the force of the blow, while another person is apprehensive and hesitant.

Recently there have been media reports about American baseball players joining Japanese teams and experiencing frustration because the emphasis and flow of the game are so different from the American version. It is the same game, with the same rules, but baseball serves a slightly different function in each culture. The same is true for Aikido. Japan's long history of martial arts produces a different experience of Aikido and Aikido training for a Japanese practioner than, say, for an American brought up in the Midwest. The result is that immersion in Japanese culture by non-Japanese is no longer imperative to understanding Aikido.

Moreover, the old culture that produced O Sensei's vision of Aikido no longer exists. Today the traditional association with martial arts is fading as younger generations of Japanese grow up less connected to Japan's martial history. Similarly in America, the pioneer experience has vanished and the gulf between New Yorkers and Midwesterners is contracting. In short, through the Internet, increasing global travel, and the inter-connectedness of national economies, the planet is quickly moving to a one-mind, one-culture world and a more cosmopolitan approach may be necessary to grasp the principles of Aikido. In the future the ability to transcend culture may be as important as physical ability for incorporating Aikido's philosophy.

Question: Some people put a lot of emphasis on the Japanese aspects of Aikido—we use Japanese terms, wear Japanese uniforms, and practice Japanese etiquette. Some practitioners even insist that if you're not Japanese, you can't really learn Aikido. How important is this Japanese perspective in learning Aikido movement?

Answer: Any person can learn Aikido. If they have the desire to learn, they can learn. For a Japanese Aikidoist, it is important to learn the Japanese martial tradition of training. For the rest of us, American or European or whatever our culture, the Japanese martial experience is not as significant. We need to draw upon our own martial traditions that stretch back thousands of years in order to understand the context of Aikido's philosophy. At the same time, though, we must respect this gift given to the world by Aikido's founder, Morehei Ueshiba.

However, consider that until World War II, only the Japanese perpetuated Aikido's legacy. Now millions of non-Japanese are also heirs to this tradition. The result is that Aikido has transcended political and cultural boundaries. In the Twenty-first Century the principles of Aikido have become like the laws of physics—they no longer have anything to do with a specific nationality, race, or tradition. People need to draw upon the historical martial conflicts as well as the cultural traditions of their own heritages in order to help understand the philosophy and movements of Aikido and place Aikido into the proper context of their lives. This point of view does not mean that we should not honor the source and origin of Aikido. In fact, it is more important than ever that we acclaim O Sensei and celebrate his philosophy. But at the same time we should not cloud our perspective of Aikido by trying to adopt the Japanese worldview if we aren't Japanese.

Question: What are some ways that the Japanese worldview differs from the American worldview?

Answer: Japan's political evolution and long martial history are important to understanding the difference between the way Japanese and Americans view the world. For over one thousand years prior to the Twentieth Century, Japan's political structure consisted of many powerful clans fighting one another. A clan's warriors, called *samurai*, could not use the same martial arts as their rivals or they would be easily defeated. The result was that the clans secretly developed many distinct martial arts in order to protect themselves. Americans have almost no experience with this kind of martial secrecy or the resulting significance of the master-student relationship.

While the cultural differences are important to understand, it isn't necessary for an American or a European to have a Japanese mindset to study Aikido. American Aikidoists should stop trying to copy the Japanese worldview, because we will never fully comprehend it. The cultures are so different psychologically and symbolically that we will never really understand each other at a deep level. The result is that trying to become "Japanese" in order to understand Aikido will only retard your own Aikido growth in the long term. In fact, for an American to eschew his own culture in favor of Japanese culture isn't particularly useful to his or her understanding of Aikido principles and movement. The possibility exists for each of us to reach O Sensei's level of understanding.

Cultural differences play a major role in how American Aikidoists interpret the outcome of specific training techniques. In most cases, a technique ends with the attacker being thrown to the ground and the defender standing over or pinning the attacker. For Americans it is hard not to view this situation as either winning or losing. It seems unlikely that Aikido could have ever been developed by a sports conscious society like America. However, this point of view is an obstacle to advanced Aikido training.

Question: One of the things that has always puzzled me is that in Aikido there is supposed to be no competition, but there is clearly winning: I throw and I win. How do you explain this contradiction?

Answer: In the beginning it looks as if there is winning or losing, since a student is always throwing her attacker in the same direction, repeating the same movement over and over again. However, at this beginning stage, Aikido partners are really falling down for each other, so it is silly to think in terms of competition, or winning and losing. This early training provides students with an opportunity to study balance and movement and to learn *ukemi* in order to fall properly without injury. This type of practice is a foundation so that students can go on to more advanced training.

Later, attacking partners become *ukemi*-conscious. This means that attackers study how to reverse the techniques applied by defenders and how to fall in order to protect themselves. The result is that, in the future, the defender applying the techniques does not always throw in the same direction. He is thinking about how to stop his partner from reversing the throw. At the same time, the attacker is moving with the receiving partner, looking for that point where she can reverse the technique. At this point in advanced training, partners are no longer thinking about winning and losing, but just adjusting to each other's movements until a technique works.

Question: Why is it that Aikido training never seems to go beyond kata into this free-flowing movement that you just described?

Answer: The simple answer is that many students cannot do the type of *ukemi* necessary for this free-flowing kind of training. *Ukemi* is not just backward-and-forward rolling. It involves moving with a partner in order to fall in any direction and on any surface to avoid injury. *Ukemi* is mastering all kinds of falls fast and hard, slow and soft; making the body flat to the mat when necessary; falling on a wooden or concrete floor. When the student can do this type of *ukemi*, then the practice evolves into a free-flowing movement where an attacker can take *ukemi* not just to reverse his partner and the partner can throw without injuring the attacker. This level of *ukemi* performance is the object of basic training.

Question: Some students believe that Aikido is an end in itself, encompassing everything there is to know in the martial arts. What do you think?

Answer: No martial art can be everything at once. Aikido has its own basic movements and basic practice is conducted within its own narrow set of rules. For example, a person is either on offense or defense, but not both. Other martial arts have similar limitations: karate students practice forms without partners; in kendo, there is no grappling; in American boxing there is no kicking; wrestling does not use weapons.

For many people martial arts and the concept of warrior arts are synonymous. Much is made these days of archetypal warrior energy which traditionally would include discipline, training, and protecting the weak and the innocent. In modern martial arts the focus is principally on training and discipline.

Question: Many books have been written about the warrior ethos in modern day society and the premise that there is warrior energy in all of us. In a larger sense this warrior energy is portrayed not only as the fighter fighting for the larger good of the community, but as the quester questing to understand his or her being. Does this warrior ethos play a role in the philosophy of *aiki* movement?

Answer: It can, but, perhaps the question you are really asking is, "Does the warrior have a place in society today?" The modern world is no longer like Europe's or Japan's feudal eras, when martial arts were used to protect oneself and one's community, and for fighting wars. Unless you are going into the military there is no place for this kind of training in modern society. And even then it is only for special-forces groups, since the majority of military and police personnel rely on weapons for combat.

But martial arts training is only a part of the warrior ethos. For example, in Aikido we are not creating fighters. Most people now understand that the martial arts are no longer just for self defense. Today martial arts training has become a means for changing ourselves.

Question: Then what is the best way to train?

Answer: Once you understand that the goal of martial arts is not to produce archetypal warriors, the best way to train then becomes subject to debate. If the purpose of training is to facilitate personal transformation, I don't believe we can fully comprehend yet what kind of training will accomplish this goal. What would work well is for students to spend perhaps two-to-three years learning basic movements and then spend several more years, pursuing intensive training. With this kind of hard training, Aikido becomes the central focus of your life. You take as many classes, seminars, and camps as you can, training your body to a peak of fitness and ability. Find training partners who can push you to your physical and psychological limits, and then past them. Once you have reached this peak, your training takes on a quality of questioning the principles of interaction inherent in Aikido.[1]

After this period of time, perhaps ten to fifteen years, people have redefined their body integration: they are more coordinated, they know many fighting techniques, their sense of time may have slowed down a bit, and their overall awareness has increased considerably.

Question: But they have not necessarily arrived at a breakthrough in functionality.

Answer: That's right. A breakthrough into a higher level of functionality is elusive. I believe Second Level Training (SLT) can move people in that direction.

Question: What is Second Level Training?

Answer: It is a set of practices, using Aikido movements and techniques, designed to increase a person's centeredness and improve a person's ability to handle conflict.

Question: Do you have to know Aikido in order to study SLT?

Answer: In fact, you don't. When Ikeda Sensei started his centering classes, many of the participants had no martial arts background. There was no falling or *ukemi* in the class, yet after a year of training, a number of students had developed significant skills to deal with power and attackers. People of all ages, abilities, and conditions can gain from Second Level Training. In some way it may be more basic than Aikido technique training since it can be used by students at any period of study—from beginner to advanced—to improve their technical ability as well as their physical power.

A new vision for martial arts, and SLT in particular, redefines the student-teacher role. The strong attachment or devotion to a particular guru or martial arts master is an anachronism and eventually gets in the way of each person fully developing his or her greatest martial arts potential. This does not mean that teachers no longer guide their students, but that there is no need to perpetuate the ancient system of instruction, in which teachers regarded their students as property.

Question: What are some of the ways martial arts have changed from the feudal era to the present?

Answer: In feudal times, whether in Europe or Asia, martial arts was the art of killing one another. In 15th century France, for example, a knight had no choice: in order to survive he had to know as many forms of fighting as possible. If he encountered an adversary who was a master of the mace,[2] he needed to be familiar with the mace or he would not know how to defend himself. That is why knights and men-at-arms in feudal Europe spent so much time studying weapons. The warrior of this age studied fighting as a full time occupation the way a modern soldier does today.

In the beginning of the Twenty-first Century, it is no longer crucial for the vast majority of Americans, Europeans, and Asians to learn martial arts for survival. Neighbors are not at war with one another; friends do not betray one another to their enemies, nor do they put each other's lives in jeopardy. Currently, several nations are poignant exceptions, but the harsh circumstances of these countries' citizens underscores the fact that a majority of Western and Asian people are more concerned with economic well-being than physical safety.

Nowadays the average urban resident has the luxury to choose a martial art based on his likes or dislikes. He can then decide whether his body can take the demands of the art and whether he has the time to devote to it. An individual can then take a lifetime to study one martial art and understand its deepest meaning and still have time for family and community obligations. However, if a student attempts to study everything—Aikido, boxing, Judo, fencing, and so on, there is not enough time to understand them at their deepest levels. The student can only have a taste of these arts, so practioners must focus their training on one art. In that way, the student fits the art and the art fits the student. This is the main difference between martial arts training today and in feudal times.

The time may come, however, when martial arts instructors will function more like Olympic-style coaches than like masters. This will likely happen as the goal of martial arts shifts from fighting skills to self realization. In the Twenty-first Century we are long past the necessity of secrecy and devotion to one master.

Aikido has raised some interesting questions about energy and power because some of the feats attributed to Aikido's founder and his disciples border on the magical.

Question: Is there some kind of power that Aikido training allows the practioner access? I'm not referring simply to muscle power but a kind of effortless power.

Answer: If by effortless, you mean *ki* power that knocks people down without touching them, that should be left to the comic books. But there is a type of effortless power that can be developed through body coordination and balance. This is part of SLT practice.

The most important component of SLT is balance: your relationship with the ground and gravity. Without balance, there is no way to focus power. All of us, as we grow up, have a certain amount of balance that we develop through the games we play as children and our everyday movements. We become accustomed to it and use it naturally. Athletes spend a lot of time working on their balance to give them even more grace, stability, and strength. In Aikido, as in athletics, we perfect our balance in order to bring more power to a throw or an attack.

Body coordination, how the body's parts work in relation to each other, is the second part of understanding effortless power. Like balance, it is something we have possessed since childhood. However, in its everyday state, body coordination is unrefined and most of its potential goes unused. Beginning Aikido students may think they are well-coordinated, but in reality most have little awareness of their body's relationship in three-dimensional space or to their partner. The result is that their hands, legs, and torsos do not move in a coordinated fashion and their power is quite weak. As I have said, basic Aikido practice develops total body coordination, which over time will be experienced by the student as increased power. Moreover, with the addition of Second Level Training, body coordination improves greatly. This feeling of increased power will become your new natural state and it will seem as though you are moving effortlessly.

Question: We've all had the experience of throws that are suddenly effortless. For some reason it is no problem to throw relatively big people. How is this possible?

Answer: This is one of the skills that can be enhanced by SLT. When the properly aligned body moves to the right place at the right time, and a center-to-center connection occurs simultaneously with a neutralization technique, a throw is possible with no more effort than if there were no attacker at all.

The magic is inherent in our bodies. It is how we train ourselves every day that makes the difference. If each day a person did some type of training, he or she would be stronger and healthier. That is what I am trying to say: discipline your mind, body, and spirit by training every day. It doesn't matter if it is Aikido; it could be any martial art, any sport. Within this context SLT is not some special power, but a means to achieve the ability to handle an attack effortlessly.

Question: Some martial artists talk about a "center intelligence" that allows them to respond successfully in fighting situations. Can you explain what this means?

Answer: Moving correctly in a fighting situation is like automatically putting your hands up to catch something that is unexpectedly thrown to you. This reaction is body memory—patterning an action into the body until it becomes innate. A student develops this kind of intelligence from practicing the same movement over and over. It takes time, like any other skill—for example, playing the piano. At first the keyboard is foreign to us and we are clumsy coordinating our finger movements with the pedals at our feet. When we begin to learn, we are forced to look at the keys repeatedly. But with practice we coordinate our hand and finger movements and adding the pedals becomes easy. After ten years we no longer notice how effortlessly our hands and fingers move across the keyboard in coordination with the pedals at our feet.

Second Level Training is similar. Though SLT may seem awkward at first, with practice and repetition a student will be able to handle an opponent smoothly without injury to himself. Like the automatic catching reflex, through experience and practice people can develop skills with the same effortless response. But, as with music, in order to produce beautiful harmonies you have to study the nuances of form and tone. Similarly in martial arts, simple repetition of techniques will never give you the ability to adjust to an opponent when he changes timing and attacks.

Section One

THE ELEMENTS OF POWER

There are many levels of training within martial arts. The most basic level introduces effective forms of movement. These movements are not extraordinary in themselves but are refinements of what the body does or can do naturally. For example, a 180-degree turn that might be accomplished awkwardly with one leg extended to maintain balance is instead compressed into a precise, fluid pivot.

The basic movement forms, or kata are practiced over and over until they are incorporated into the body and become the foundation for the martial art one is studying. These movements can be short and simple or arranged in long sequences, involving many hand, arm, and foot positions.

In Aikido these basic movement forms are expressed as techniques, involving variations on joint locks, and hip and projection throws. Within all of Aikido's basic techniques, balance, body alignment, and effective motion are being developed. However, many students never progress past the first level of movement, nor do they initiate a serious investigation of the concepts of balance, body alignment, and motion in order to develop a deeper understanding of them. For some students, these basic movement abilities are viewed more like the skills of a figure skater or basketball player. That is, they are a means to an end, such as winning tournaments, a good workout, stress reduction, greater self-esteem, and participation in the martial arts fantasy of power over others.

This first section of Center: The Power of Aikido moves beyond basic movement and explores the second level of training: an investigation into the nature and source of power. In martial arts, power is the integration of the entire body with the mind in order to form a complete, focused, and conscious movement. In Aikido, we create power by unifying the body from the feet to the tips of the fingers. As we fuse ourselves into a single unit, the power within us grows and expands. Finally this unity extends to our minds so that both mind and body work together.

In this section, we introduce the concept of power, then discuss its four elements.

1. *Centeredness:* Hara, seika tanden, and center are words used to describe that part of the human body, located below the navel, where power is stored before being directed elsewhere. A broader sense of center includes the whole body's standing balance in relationship to the ground. Developed over time through rigorous training, this concept of center, or "centeredness," allows a martial artist to transform an opponent's power into his own. In addition, centeredness, or centering, can also be described as a state of being that allows one to move and act reflectively instead of reactively.

2. **Relaxation:** Relaxation is more than just the opposite of being stiff or tense. It is a necessary condition in order to create power in Aikido. Basically, relaxing means you can use your whole body centeredness, first, to receive the power of your partner's attack and redirect it into the ground, and second, to return your own power one hundred percent for the technique.

3. **Alignment:** Alignment creates a physical pathway within your body from the hands and head through the feet into the ground in order to channel an opponent's attack into the ground and return your own power from the ground.

4. **Connection:** Connection links your physical center with your opponent's. It creates a power line that allows you to feel your opponent's intent and to unbalance as well as to control her.

The problem with discussing the elements of power in separate chapters is that they are not separate at all. It is only for the purposes of trying to explain them that we have chosen to differentiate them. In practice, each element combines with the others to form effective applications of physical *power. Readers will quickly discover that the elements of power are so inte-grated that if one of them is taken out of the mix, the others lose much of their potential.*

Finally, aside from the practical aspect of becoming a more powerful martial artist, the study of the elements of power is important because as one progresses in one's training, one becomes freer. A wider range of move-ment becomes increasingly possible at each succeeding moment until "bat-tle" evolves into play. It seems possible that this new freedom in the form of changes on the mat transfers to life in general. In a powerful sense, freedom can be defined as "unrestricted or not constricted." As many philosophers have observed, the experience of life for a free person is different than that for the constricted or restricted person. When you live a restricted life, the main theme is struggle. However, the free person allows life to come to him or her. Secure in this power, he or she has a greater ability to hear the rhythm of life and move to it.

Chapter 1

POWER

One of the characteristics that differentiates martial arts from most other skilled physical activities is that, at its core, it employs techniques which direct destructive force, or power, from one person to another. Through a process of physical contact, an attacker attempts to kill, render unconscious, injure, immobilize, or dislodge an opponent. Or, put more simply, it is physical pressure applied by one body on another.

Of course, not all physical pressure of one body against another is an attack. For example, a child just learning to walk is toppled over by a well-intentioned kiss. Yet even in this example, the same principles apply.

As we grow up, we all become moderately skilled at adjusting to various kinds of power relationships. The bump on a crowded street causes most of us only minor discomfort while we retain our balance. On the other hand, some football players show a remarkable ability to absorb powerful blows with little or no effect; in many cases the tacklers end up on the ground.

In Aikido, some of the primary properties of power are: 1) it can increase, 2) it can become stronger and manifest in various ways, 3) another person's power can be received in a non-damaging way, 4) an attacking person's power can be used to make the receiver stronger, and 5) an attacking person's power can be used against him or her.

In basic Aikido training, students learn simple methods to deal with power. Yet, through training in the elements of power presented in this book, seemingly magical results can be achieved.

One of the most important aspects of power training is to shift from the mode of using an isolated part of the body to perform a task, to using the whole body to perform the same task.

Question: What is the relationship between whole-body movement and power?

Answer: In every day life you do not need to use whole body movement to accomplish most physical tasks. For example if you have to pick up something light, such as a fork, it is easy to do so using only your fingers. If the object you are trying to lift is heavier, you have to use your hand or perhaps your arms; heavier still and you add your legs. In a sense, we know visually how much of our body we have to use. We know that we can pick up a fork with our fingers and that we have to add the use of our legs to pick up a cinder block.

In Aikido, however, we don't want to rely on this visually induced tendency that divides our body movements into finger power, arm power, leg power and so on. Instead, anytime we are doing Aikido we must focus on using our whole body, integrating our hands, arms, upper body, and legs into a single unit.

Many people in Aikido continue making a judgment about size and weight thinking, "this is a small person so I only have to use my arm to throw him or her to the mat;" or "this is big person so I have to use leg power instead of just my arms." To develop whole body power, you have to abandon this way of thinking. When working with partners—moving them and executing a technique—you must use your entire body the whole time, regardless of their size and weight.

A clue for understanding the above concept is that it may take one hundred percent of a person's arm power to throw an attacker, but only 15 percent of full-body power.

Question: Does this mean that in practice we should use full power when training with everyone?

Answer: You have to vary the amount and learn to adjust your power with training. However, you do not adjust the use of power by reducing or eliminating the use of some part of your body. You still must use your whole body when training. Simply move in accordance with the abilities of the partner you are working with. For example, don't throw with full force in a light training situation. But that does not mean using only your hands and arms. All of the power employed comes from a unified body and center. "Full power" doesn't mean just throwing someone really hard into the mat. Rather, a more descriptive definition of "full power" is using your power fully, even in a slow, controlled movement. When working with beginners, move slowly, but still use your entire body and your center to derive the power. Please don't confuse throwing forcefully with training at full power.

Receiving an attacker's power is akin to the shift a person makes from a relaxed standing position when playing catch with a heavy medicine ball. When the person receives the medicine ball, her relaxed state shifts as she directs the force of the throw through her legs into the ground. By doing this, her power and balance are increased over the standing, relaxed position.

Question: Can you tell us what happens when you receive an opponent's power?

Answer: I receive an opponent's power in such a way that it strengthens my balance, otherwise the attacker's power will unbalance me and I will be knocked down. For example, if I am standing on a moving subway and the train suddenly stops or turns, I will then lose my balance and fall to one side. So, when the subway stops suddenly, I have to catch its power and direct it through my body to reinforce my connection to the ground. In this manner I will not be unbalanced and knocked down.

It is the same when being attacked. First, my ordinary, or standing balance—when I am merely standing without anything pressing on me from any direction is different than when someone attacks me. This standing balance allows me to walk and move, even to run easily. When someone attacks me, his power, like the subway's sudden stop, is trying to knock me down. I have to adjust myself to receive my attacker's power in such a way that this power automatically is directed into the ground.

This will make my balance stronger. The better I can do this, the stronger my center becomes.

One method to demonstrate this idea is to stand on one leg. This is difficult to do for a long period of time without losing your balance and falling over. But if you can reach out with one finger and touch the wall, then it is easy to keep your balance. You must use your opponent's attack the same way as you would use the wall. You catch your opponent's power to make a "third leg" to reinforce your balance.

Question: When you are receiving an opponent's power, where is your focus?

Answer: My focus is on where the power from my opponent's attack is directed. Maybe it is a pull or maybe it is a push; perhaps he is striking me. In a split second, I have to determine where my opponent's attack is directed. If I do this successfully, then at first touch my opponent's power will be directed into the ground without breaking my own balance. In this way I can establish what I call a "power-to-power relationship" with my opponent; that is to say, a connection with my whole body to my opponent's body.[3] The Japanese refer to this as *musubi* or *ittai*, meaning mutual body.

Question: What happens to his power after you receive it?

Answer: After I receive my opponent's power and it has been shunted into the ground, I return it through my body to apply a technique. But the application of technique is different than using my opponent's power to strengthen my balance. In strengthening my balance, I use my partner's power to increase my ground connection and weaken his. His power is then linked to my own power and if I move, he moves with me. In doing this, I have broken his balance and I can then apply a technique that is appropriate.

Question: So Second Level Training students should always receive their partner's power in order to catch it and use it?

Answer: This concept should become a part of regular practice. In fact, during advanced training, students should study how to use their partner's power: to receive it, catch it, ground it, and then connect it to their own power in order to break their partner's balance and be able to apply a technique that they already know from basic practice.

Resisting with only the muscles of his shoulder and forearm, the defender is forced off balance by the attacker's push.

Defender channels this power from the wrist, through the arm, to the center and through the legs straight into the ground to strengthen his balance.

The defender is pulled off balance by the attacker.

Defender channels this power from the wrist, through the arm, to the center and through the legs straight into the ground to strengthen his balance.

For example, if an attacker grabs your wrist and pushes or pulls it in order to break your balance, channel this power—by directing it through your skeletal structure—from the wrist, through the arm, to the center, and straight into the ground to strengthen your balance. The opponent's power is then naturally brought back up from the ground; that is, your legs spring back from the ground. This is similar to using the compression force created by a trampoline pushing upward through your legs to your center. From there, direct this power to the attacker's center and then to one side, breaking his balance and making him weaker.[4] From this point your movement continues into *shihonage, kokyunage, iriminage,* or whatever martial arts technique is appropriate.

Using your partner's power to make yourself stronger is the essence of Second Level Training. Of course, in real fighting situations, movements, such as ducking, are also useful in handling an attacker.

The concept of power and its elements that is being discussed in this book is not the same as the common notion of ki.

Question: Returning to the topic of power, some martial arts practioners believe that the ground is full of *ki* and that they are pulling this power out of the ground to throw their attackers. Is this at all possible?

Answer: The ground does not provide special power to us. Instead, it is our bodies that are important. Let me use the example of pushing a car. Notice that when pushing a car you are the link between the car and the ground, just as you are the link between the attacker and the ground. You do not pull something special out of the ground to push the car, which is not to say that the ground isn't important, but we can't do anything to manipulate it. We can only adjust ourselves. If you have positioned and aligned your body correctly, you will naturally channel the force of an attack into the ground and back to your attacker. The ground is not special; it is the position and alignment of your body in receiving the force of the attack that are important.

Question: We've talked a lot about our partner's power and receiving it. Let's now explore building up your own power. How do you create your power?

Answer: I have used my training to learn how to unify my whole body. In this way my legs, my upper body, and my arms are not working separately, but as a unit.

Another way to look at it is to say that through practice I have learned slowly that the way to create my own power is to connect my whole self. A big part of martial arts training is the building up of all these connections within my body.

Like most beginners, I tried moving my partners with only my arms. However, my techniques were weak and I could not move more advanced partners at all. Then I learned to add my upper body, followed by hips and legs. I became stronger and my partners could not move me as easily. Connections within my body were beginning to link together, thicken, and become stronger. My power became progressively greater. My techniques became more effective and I was harder and harder to unbalance. Until finally my entire body was linked together and I was naturally connected to the ground.

Question: Is there any end to this?

Answer: I believe only time can stop this building up of power derived from integrating your body. As long as you are alive and your mind and spirit are focused you can continue to grow. It is a little bit like developing a muscle. As you exercise it, more and more strands of muscle fiber are added to it. It becomes bigger and stronger. There is no limit to the number of connections you can make.

The more you integrate yourself, the more connections you make to link up your entire body, the better you can generate whole-body power to move and throw your attacker.

One interesting way to look at this is to notice that the nature of this type of power changes as we grow older. It can become stronger even though our muscle strength diminishes. This is why in Aikido older people often easily handle younger and bigger attackers.

**_Training exercises directed at developing your power
and improving your power relationships with training partners._**

*Defender places her elbow against her hip, allowing the force of the attacker's push
to be directed through her hip bones and her legs into the ground.*

*Defender concentrates on her forward leg and bends her forward knee, directing
the force of defender's pull through the forward leg and into the ground.*

Defender lightly rests her palms on attacker's elbows and her own elbows against her torso channeling the force of attacker's push through her pelvic girdle, down her legs and into the earth.

The defender slides forward from her center uprooting the attacker.

Question: Let's go back to handling an attacker's power. What practices do you advocate?

Answer: The first one is learning to feel your partner. For example, when a training partner grabs your wrist and pushes or pulls, focus on feeling the direction and power of the attack. At the same time, consciously begin directing your partner's power through your arm, upper body, and hips to your legs and into the ground. In this way you start to establish the connection between your partner's attack and the ground. You are also building a stronger link between your hand and the ground. Do not be disappointed if this takes a while to learn. Use your mind and your spirit to focus on this practice.

Question: Are there any suggestions that will help with this first step?

Answer: In this first step you and your partner have to work together. You have to trust one another.

Secondly, you are establishing a power relationship with your partner. By this I mean that you are creating a pathway or connection from the ground beneath your partner's feet to the ground beneath your feet. It is like a rope. If it is slack, then the pathway has a gap in it and there is no connection. If your partner is only squeezing your wrist, then you have to take the slack out. Either you can push forward a little bit or pull back a little bit to feel the connection. This way if you move, your partner will move.

Question: What is the next step?

Answer: Developing your body so that it naturally connects to the ground and this kind of power comes spontaneously. This is why every class has to be more than just falling down and getting up. That kind of practice is just physical exercise. If you want to build up your power, if you want to forge the links connecting your entire body together as one unit and improve your power relationships, then you have to use your mind to study the ground-to-ground relationship between you and your partner, and the connections that make for whole-body movement. Skill at Second Level Training cannot be achieved by mere rote repetition of techniques.

Question: We have talked a lot about receiving power using examples of wrist grabs. What about strikes, such as punches to the face?

Answer: The principles are the same as in receiving the opponent's attack in the form of a wrist grab. We move in relation to our partner so that we are in the optimal place to channel his power into the ground with our whole body. The safest way to do that is with an initial contact through the arm. Eventually, with enough practice, you will be able to receive the full force of a 220-pound person's attack in such a way that your opponent appears to bounce off you.

However, since the principles are the same for either wrist grabs or strikes, wrist grabs should be used initially because it is easier to learn and demonstrate the relationship of power between ourselves and our partners.

Chapter 2

CENTEREDNESS

Center is the key principle in SLT's concept of Aikido training. While Aikido's movements, techniques, and ukemi *are largely what differentiate it from other martial arts, Aikido's center development has much to offer all arts, as well as any activity employing movement skills.*

In the martial arts, "center" is a concept that has many interpretations. Aikido recognizes one common perception of center as an area in the middle of the body slightly below the navel called the hara *or* seika tanden. *In Eastern philosophy, and therefore in the martial arts, this point takes on numinous properties. Most martial arts instructors share some or all of these beliefs. In particular, Aikido teachers will often talk about the* seika tanden *as the source of energy for all activities. However, the kind of center one is building with Second Level Training is different than the common Eastern philosophical notion and is in some ways more elusive. Indeed, SLT moves beyond just the physical placement of center and refers to a much broader concept we call "centeredness."*

There does not seem to be any single word that clearly defines the idea of centeredness. The psychological notion of wholeness captures some of the meaning of centeredness as does a heightened state of athletic prowess sometimes described as "the zone." All of us have witnessed examples of "the zone" in sports: the perfect pass from quarterback to receiver, or the blind pass between teammates on the basketball court. This kind of centeredness is at once a state of being and a set of physical skills. However, while the means by which one develops centeredness vary from one physical skill activity to another, the centeredness that emerges from martial arts training appears to carry over into life in general.

In what follows, we clarify the distinction between Second Level Training's centeredness and the seika tanden. *We have tried to use throughout this book the terms* seika tanden *and* hara *exclusively to mean the physical center of the body, i.e., that point below the navel.*

Question: Many Aikidoists talk about center as the gravitational center of the human body. What is center for you?

Answer: Physically, what Americans refer to as the center, the Chinese call the *dan tien* and the Japanese call the *seika tanden*. Located about one inch below the navel, the *seika tanden* is the point where, according to ancient traditions, one's power resides. The Japanese call this place the *seika tanden* because all energy comes from here; all energy received from an attacker is stored here; and all energy for movement or throwing is discharged from here. However, the idea of centeredness is stability and balance—physical, mental, and spiritual. And in martial arts all balance and stability derive from movement.

Question: This somewhat confusing. Are you saying that without movement there is no center?

Answer: One way to imagine "centeredness" is that like the skeleton that supports the muscles of your body, "centeredness" is a living framework that supports life. For example, when you are sick, your framework for supporting life is incapacitated and you are unable to do very much. You might say that your centeredness is weak or depleted. Particularly, you can't run or engage in sports activity at an efficient level because it is very difficult to move with any kind of balance.

It is clear that humans are always experimenting with centeredness beyond what is required to stand, walk, and run. In fact, much of what we admire in dance and sport, and pay big dollars to see, is unusual centeredness or centeredness under stress.

Question: In class, when told to become more centered, most students will do something such as stand up straighter. What is meant by becoming more centered?

Answer: The first thing required in becoming centered is in fact to stand up straight. This means to be more balanced. For example, if you stand on your tiptoes, you can balance yourself. Basketball players know how to maintain their balance jumping and shooting. However, it is not very balanced from a martial arts point of view. This is because if your partner attacks, you don't have the proper center—the balance or stability—to receive his energy and therefore you will be knocked down. In martial arts we have to develop centeredness a little differently than say a basketball player.

Mind is important to centeredness; that is, where you place your attention when performing physical skills. Elite athletes have learned that awareness can be controlled and specifically focused to achieve athletic excellence. However, the minds of most non-athletes tend to run helter skelter during physical activity and bringing awareness to the seika tanden *for an extended period of time is not something most non-athletes have experienced. Controlling and focusing awareness is necessary to develop greater centeredness in the martial arts.*

Question: In martial arts what are you developing when you develop your center?

Answer: To me it is developing my mind. Centeredness is, of course, physical but it is also the mind. For example, you must put your awareness in your feet so that your energy goes into the ground. If your awareness is only in your head, you will be less stable.

Question: It seems to me that you are describing visualization—seeing energy come down to the ground and aligning your body to the ground in order to be centered. Is that true?

Answer: Yes. You must use your imagination. If your awareness is always in the upper part of your body, in your shoulders, neck, and head, your balance will be different than if your awareness is in the lower part of your body. Ballet dancers, figure skaters, and basketball players create a balance that is directed upward so that they can leave the ground more easily. They are centered for what they do, which is to be able to leap off the ground and perform feats in the air and still stay balanced.

Martial artists are oriented in the opposite direction. They use the ground for power, so their balance is directed downward into their legs, and their feet must be connected to the ground, thereby producing a different feeling of centeredness than that of a ballet dancer.

Question: Is there any kind of physical sensation from your head down to the ground?

Answer: No, nothing like *ki* flows through my body. It is really just an awareness or how I focus my mind. What I prefer to look for are ways to improve my martial balance or centeredness. One simple way is, if you bend your knees. That typically makes your whole body better connected to the ground. Most martial arts rely on bending the knees a little bit so that the body's weight is directed through the legs into the ground.

Question: We've observed an exercise where one person puts his arm in front of him and another person tries to walk through it. The first time, the person walking places his attention in his head and he cannot walk through the outstretched arm. The second time, the person puts his attention in his *seika tanden* and he is able to walk through effortlessly. What is happening in this exercise?

Answer: This exercise illustrates that centeredness mostly involves developing the mind and demonstrates how important the mind is to centeredness.

Question: So you believe that awareness can be moved down out of the head into the *seika tanden*?

Answer: Yes.

Question: Most Westerners think of their awareness being in their brains or behind their eyes. In other words, it is centered in the senses located in the head. We don't think of putting our awareness in our centers. How would this work in daily life?

Answer: If you want to turn and look at someone, and if you want to keep a high level of centeredness, then you should consider that your movement is originating from your *seika tanden* instead of just turning your face toward him. The problem, from a martial arts perspective, is that if only the head moves, there is a disconnection between your whole body and your head, and that creates a weakness. That means your power is reduced because your body is not maximally integrated.

For example, in Aikido when we practice the technique *iriminage*[5], your partner can be very strong and his balance very good, but if you twist his head to the side, he will become weaker and easier to move. So it is with you. When you are moving, use your mind to put your awareness in your *seika tanden* and see what happens.

Question: Do you place your awareness in your *seika tanden*?

Answer: That's just part of it. Basically my awareness is within my entire body because it is all linked together.[6] This is an internal aspect of *musubi*.[7]

Beginners have to practice placing their awareness in their *seika tanden* and moving their whole body, including the head, with the *seika tanden*. The *seika tanden* links the body's movements together to produce full-body awareness. There is great power in this possibility.

Question: When we talked about power, we also talked about linking the body together and making connections between the legs, body, arms, and hands. It sounds as though centeredness is a similar concept—linking one's awareness with the *seika tanden*, body, legs, and the ground. Is centeredness just another level of building connections within one's body?

Answer: Yes, but it is important to remember that beginners can't try to build everything at the same time or achieve a lifetime of experience in a few short months. The beginner must first work on just placing awareness in the *seika tanden* during simple movement exercises.

Question: Is that what you mean by "working on center?"

Answer: Yes. "Working on center" is the practice of placing your awareness in your *seika tanden* in order to build up standing and moving balance in relation to an attacking force. Extending this discipline to the example of walking through the arm that was mentioned previously, we observe that in order to walk through the arm, one must "walk from the center of the body." Walking from center is a simple example of working on center, yet it is also the basis of every movement we do in the martial arts. Wherever we move, our seika tanden goes first. Eventually, through thoughtful practice, moving from the *seika tanden* becomes the natural way of moving.

Question: What other exercises can students do to help build center?

Answer: One exercise is *funakoki undo,* or what we Americans call a rowing exercise. In *funakoki undo* the legs are in a triangle stance with either foot forward. Weight is shifted back and forth from one leg to the other so that the arms swing naturally in front of the waist. With this rowing movement you shift your center, your balance, from the back foot to the front foot and back again. This develops and strengthens balance.

Funakoki undo

Ikkyo undo

Ikkyo undo is the same rowing movement, but this time swinging the arms upward to shoulder height. This exercise helps students learn centeredness when the upper body is involved in the movement.

Question: What would be an example of an exercise for developing centeredness with a partner?

Answer: In Aikido we have *tenkan* and *irimi* practice at the beginning of each class. In both practices, your partner is grabbing your wrist so that you develop your center while someone is holding onto you.

Another practice would be *Tai Chi Chuan's* "push hands." In this practice, you and your partner are moving back and forth while in contact with each other. This movement develops balance in the presence of an attacking force. In addition, because you are using your hands, it connects the upper body with the lower body. This exercise aids in learning to connect the legs, body, and arms into one unit as a way to develop more power, which is what I talked about earlier.

Tenkan Practice

The attacker grasps the defender's wrist firmly.

The defender then pushes forward slightly forcing the attacker's elbow into his center and rocking him backwards and off balance.

Defender pivots in a tankan motion while keeping her own hand and defender's hand in front of her seika tanden.

The defender completes the pivot centered and balanced while the attacker is off balance.

Irimi Practice

Attacker grasps defender's wrist firmly.

The defender turns the attacker by pressing forward and forcing her elbow into her center.

The defender slides beside the attacker.

Keeping his own wrist and attacker's wrist in front of his seika tanden, *the defender twists the attacker's torso so that she is even more off balance.*

This is why *funakoki undo*, the rowing movement, and *ikkyo undo* are so important. They are gentle movements, but they integrate hand, body, and legs to increase balance and help increase power.

Question: What are the basic center movements?

Answer: Basic center movements are the same for all martial arts: 1) walking and/or sliding forward and back; 2) moving the whole body down and up; 3) pivoting in a circle; and 4) spiraling up and spiraling down. All of these basic movements should be done with awareness focused in the *seika tanden.*

Question: Is there an appropriate way to practice these basic center movements?

Answer: I have noticed that in Aikido many students, especially beginners, do not practice these basic movements appropriately, that is, with the body integrated as a whole unit. To be effective martial artists, we must learn to perform these basic movements with an integrated body. The purpose of whole-body integration is to improve the functionality of these basic movements. The function of sliding backward and forward, for example, is to change the distance relationship between you and your partner. In closing the distance between partners by either punching or using a wrist grab, most students simply lean their bodies forward, instead of sliding the whole body toward their partner. This produces an ineffective grab or punch.

In Aikido we work on each of the above basic movements separately. As I said before, you cannot work on all of these basic movements at once, because there are too many of them to concentrate on. You must work on each one separately at first, and then, like a rising tide that lifts all boats, they become stronger until everything integrates between your body and your movements when responding to an attack.

*One's centeredness is different from pure muscle strength and mass.
Simply put, centeredness can overcome large mass and muscle strength in
an opponent.*

Question: Much Aikido practice is focused on the movements used to
throw our partners rather than center training. Is center training really
important for performing techniques?

Answer: Here is why it is important. If we are receiving an attack and if
we are bigger than our partners, we can usually push them around. But
if we are the same size or if our partner is bigger than we are, our partner can push us around. The movements that make up typical Aikido
techniques just won't do it for us. That is why we have to train our centers to receive our partner's power so that it is channeled into the
ground. In other words, we can make the attacker dependent upon us for
balance. Once this action has been accomplished, we can more easily
move a bigger person and apply a technique to him or her.

Question: Does it matter where you first feel this power?

Answer: If I have full-body awareness like I talked about before, it doesn't
matter where the attack occurs. Even though my partner grabs my shoulder, or elbow, or wrist, or if he strikes me, since I have an awareness of
my body in its three dimensional state, with each part connected to the
seika tanden, I feel the attack in my center. I can feel the direction, intent,
and intensity of the attack as if it had been directed full-bore at my center. An important point is that if I try to stop the attack where the contact first occurs, it may overwhelm me. It is better to let the attacker's
power flow to my center and then deal with it.

Receiving my partner's power is also related to timing and position.
If I stand still while my partner grabs my wrist, though I may feel his
power in my center, my partner may be able to grab my center and disrupt my balance in order to control me. To avoid this, I must learn how
to move to the right position with proper timing to receive my partner's
attack so that it is I who control the power relationship.

Question: Does it matter if your partner grabs strongly or weakly?

Answer: If my partner grabs strongly, I feel his power in my center immediately. But if someone has a very weak attack, though I feel it on my skin, it is not very powerful, and does not reach my center. In this case, I have to add my own power to make the center-to-center power connection.

Question: When we are practicing together and you grab my wrist, it feels as if you are holding all of me immobile. Is that what you were talking about earlier when you said your partner may be able to grab your center and control you?

Answer: When many people grab they just hold the wrist; when I grab I take the center. I do this because martial arts is not just exercise. As an attacker it is my job is to stop my partner's movement. This makes a great difference in an attack. Taking my partner's center is kind of like the opposite of alignment.[8] I want to break down my partner's balance, then, since my partner is unbalanced and cannot align his body with the ground, he has reduced power. Therefore it is very difficult for him to move against my attack.

Usually in practice attackers merely grab their partners' wrists. This kind of grab is a beginner's attack. Later in training, just grabbing the wrist—but not the center—is comparable to a workout. At some point the training should change. However, by this time, many students will often have a lot invested in looking good and having their training partners, as it were, simply take a fall for them.

Let's go back to what I said earlier. Centeredness is not just physical training. It is more mental training than training the physical body. If you just exercise, exercise, exercise all the time, centeredness will not result, because centeredness is based on a particular kind of relationship. If this were not true, we could develop martial centeredness by doing the tango.

One of the main differences between center power, and muscle power and mass, is that while it is easy to build up the latter two in isolation, one must have an attacking force from a partner to study and build up centeredness to its fullest extent.

Question: Some martial artists maintain that balance within movement requires merely shifting weight.

Answer: Perhaps when you are training by yourself balance within movement is weight shift. When you are training alone, you have only your own two legs to maintain your balance and ground connection. However, Aikido training is always with a partner. You connect your center to your partner's and then you have four legs to maintain your centeredness. Two things happen when I receive an attack. I break down my attacker's centeredness and I use his power and his center to make my centeredness stronger. If done correctly, this happens naturally as a result of the center-to-center power connection. In free play or a fight, this happens swiftly, but we can slow it down in practice.

Question: Is there any limit to developing centeredness?

Answer: It never really ends. Developing centeredness is different than other types of training, since it encompasses: mind, *seika tanden* and full body awareness, movement, and body alignment in relation to the ground and an attacking force. As long as we can think, as long as we can move, we can build our centeredness. Eventually centeredness does not require your entire focus anymore. Because it has already developed to a certain point, it takes over and begins to guide your life. After that, you don't have to concentrate on it as fiercely anymore. Whatever you are doing—working, walking or gardening—centeredness automatically is growing stronger, affecting the way you deal with the world.

Chapter 3

RELAXATION

In Aikido, if your practice is not going well, for example, you are getting hit or are failing to throw a partner, teachers invariably say, "Relax." One of the beauties of second-level Aikido training is that through the repetition of attacks and throws it is actually possible to become relaxed enough to study a particular attack and the effectiveness of your response. Furthermore, when you change your response to the attack, you receive immediate feedback on the effectiveness of your adjustment. More often than not, if you relax, something automatically happens to change the situation, but if you remain tense, you cannot let go and nothing will change.

At a certain point in martial arts training, simply trying harder reaches a point of no return. Instead, one must relax in order to change one's timing, or understand the power relationships at play, or feel how your own body's alignment is breaking down. Within this relaxed state new possibilities emerge. Relaxation is not useful in itself, but allows other possibilities to arise.

There are many methods of relaxation and many books about relaxation for the interested reader. We have observed that two effective methods of relaxation are to breathe deeply to the ringing of a bell in order to calm the mind, or to train to the point of exhaustion. The first method, concentrating on the sound of the bell, allows students to focus their breath and their awareness in the center and let go of the chaotic process of the mind. In the second method, the student trains so hard and exhaustingly that he is forced to give up body tension and forget mental games and processes. In many instances, when a student is at the point of exhaustion and stays at this edge for a long while, he or she transcends the mind. which is telling the body it is tired and moves into a relaxed state where insight and change are possible.

Question: Define relaxation in terms of martial arts.

Answer: Relaxed alertness is the type of relaxation used in the martial arts. It embodies both mental and physical aspects, keeping the mind composed and aware, and the body's muscles loose and ready to move. A composed mind enables you to make good decisions. A relaxed body enables you to move smoothly and effortlessly. When either one is diminished, you cannot think or act effectively.

For example, if you are not relaxed when you practice, you end up relying on your muscular power to execute movements and techniques.[9] Therefore, to be successful, you have to be stronger than whomever you are training with. But this is not the only way to be successful in a martial arts sense. By being relaxed, your body can move as a unit and you are able to access power from the ground through your *seika tanden*. Second, a relaxed state allows you to be aware of the true spatial relationship between you and your attacker.

If you are relaxed, which does not mean that your muscles are limp or your mind is unfocused, you automatically move to the correct place to receive your partner's attack. In practice often people are so desperate to throw their partners that even before they receive their partner's attack they are already trying to throw their attacker. They have no idea how much force their partner's attack has or what direction it is taking. As a result, they make bad decisions and are overwhelmed by their partner's attack. Relaxation, in the sense I have been discussing it, brings about the conditions for this to change.

It is similar in day-to-day living. For example: someone has a job interview and is upset about it, perhaps even panicked about answering the questions correctly. When the interviewer asks questions, the interviewee, unable to sense the direction of the questions or the intent of the interviewer, will answer without thinking, with the result that the answers provided will not be very good.

However, if the interviewee is relaxed, it means he or she can listen well and give good answers to the questions. Aikido practice is the same. We have to be relaxed so we can feel the power of our partner and his or her intent.

Question: You mention there is a kind of power that occurs when relaxing, as opposed to tensing up. How does this happen?

Answer: Relaxation allows you to use your body as an integrated unit at any time.[10] That means your legs, body, arms, and hands work together to move and to apply a technique. In this way, you have 100 percent of your power available at all times. When the body's muscles are not relaxed, they become tense and the individual muscle groups are isolated, sometimes even working against each other. When this happens, your overall power and freedom of movement are greatly reduced.

For example, if your arm is already tense as a result of using your muscles to contract it or extend it, then you will block the rest of your body's ability to integrate it into a full range of movement possibilities. In a real sense you are in a weakened state.

Besides restricting your freedom of movement, stiffness also makes your movement very slow. European sword masters have always instructed fencing students to relax their shoulders in order to parry and thrust faster. If the shoulders and forearms are tight, then the movement of the sword will be very slow. During Europe's post-feudal era—from the 17th to the 19th centuries—if a swordsman was a half second slow, or even less, he would be killed.

Question: Let's go in another direction. Tensing the body to respond to an attack is a natural human instinct, part of the fight-or-flight response to danger. But now you are saying this response is misguided.

Answer: Yes, most especially in a fighting situation. Only the relaxed body can receive the power of an attack in such a way that it goes from contact, to center, to ground, and back to the attacker automatically. Relaxation is necessary in order to receive your partner's power correctly. By that I mean to absorb your partner's power and use it to make your power stronger. What happens when your muscles are tense is that you cannot feel your partner's power in your center, so you cannot understand or sense the true nature of the attack and you will not be able to respond appropriately. For example, when your opponent strikes and you receive the attack on your forearm, if you are tense, you are unable to feel your opponent's power in your center. You feel it only in your arm. Moreover, the strike overpowers you.

| *When defender's muscles are tense, she feels her attacker's strike only in her arm and is knocked off balance.* | *When relaxed, the defender is able to feel the attacker's power in her center and channel the strike into the ground. By moving forward she unbalances her attacker.* |

Question: Are you relaxed throughout a *kokyunage* technique?[11]

Answer: Yes, but I am still using my power. Of course, using power at this point does not mean tensing my muscles, but maintaining my structural integrity so that the power flows from the ground connection, through my *seika tanden* in the direction of my technique. It is important that you do not tense up while applying a technique, because the less relaxed you are, the greater the advantage the attacker will have, since you have created an opening or a weakness he or she can exploit.

Question: Is there always a way to perform Aikido and stay relaxed?

Answer: If you practice long enough. It comes back to experience: in the beginning, everyone uses muscle power to apply techniques and people can see that. But more experienced people, like Frank Doran Sensei or Mary Heiny Sensei, appear not to be using any muscle at all, yet they are very powerful.

For example, practicing *tenkan* following a wrist grab.[12] When new students first learn this technique, their movements are muscular but they look awkward. It also takes a long time in a martial sense for them to perform the action. But as students gain experience, the amount of time necessary to perform *tenkan* shrinks and it appears that they are not using muscle power; and in actuality they are not. Because they are more relaxed, they are no longer fighting with their partners.

Moving in this direction is one of the main goals of training. I don't see any end to it.

Chapter 4

ALIGNMENT

The least-complex explanation of alignment is the use of the body's skeleton as an internal framework to create a physical pathway within the body from the hands to the ground. The importance of proper alignment cannot be discounted. Unless you establish correct alignment from the ground to your opponent, your opponent will be able break your balance.

Alignment requires "training the body, from foot to hand, as a true unit. For instance, even turning a doorknob involves a real connection from hand to back through hip and leg to supporting foot. A recognizable portion of the power [required] to turn the doorknob comes from the torso muscles, supported by the continuous ground-strength to the hand."[13]

Proper body alignment is a principle that instructors should teach from day one of martial arts training but rarely do. In the internal arts, like Aikido, students develop bad alignment habits because training partners often give in to the defenders, giving them a false sense of power.

Alignment creates a physical pathway between your body and the ground by utilizing the body's skeletal framework and just enough muscle strength for proper posture. In the martial arts, muscle tension weakens and disrupts the body-to-ground connection. So, in order to maximize the inherent power in this connection, the practitioner needs to link the body's entire skeletal structure from the hands and head through the feet to the ground in a flexible direct line. This linkage is called alignment. The postural muscles connecting the joints must be relaxed and used with no more effort than that needed to maintain the skeleton's internal structure. If this alignment is disrupted, then the pathway to the ground is broken and the

Aikidoist cannot use ground-strength so the only available power will be whatever strength is inherent in the arm or shoulder.

Saotome Sensei, a personal student of O Sensei for fifteen years, has always stressed proper body alignment. He is the perfect model of what proper body alignment should look like.

Defender's entire skeletal structure needs to be linked from the hands and head through the feet into the ground during the course of the counter throw.

Attacker grabs defender's wrist in a two hand yonkyo grip and forces her off balance.

Defender realigns her body and her arm so that the attacker cannot apply the yonkyo.

Maintaining alignment to the ground, defender slides forward, forcing the attacker's elbow into the air.

The defender then adjusts alignment so that she is applying ikkyo to the attacker by using the power of her legs to move forward.

However, while it is a relatively simple matter for a skilled martial artist to demonstrate alignment, it is very difficult for the beginning student to maintain this state under the stress of an attack. In fact, many beginners' failures to execute techniques effectively result from improper body alignment. While these failures often look like breakdowns in technique, in reality they are simple alignment problems.

Question: What is alignment?

Answer: Alignment is the relationship of all parts of the body to themselves and the ground. In a postural sense, alignment is standing straight, balanced and weight evenly distributed between both legs. Another facet of alignment relates to the center-to-center connection with partners and will be discussed more fully in Chapter Five on Connection.

Question: When you align your body what are you thinking about?

Answer: Standing up straight, maintaining balance and distributing my weight evenly in my legs.

Question: When your partner attacks and you have taken his power into your body, where do you put it?

Answer: First into my wrist, or wherever my partner is grabbing or striking. From there it follows a pathway within my body, through my *seika tanden*, to the ground. This pathway is the alignment I defined earlier.

Question: Would you describe what this pathway is and how it relates to alignment?

Answer: One way to depict alignment is by visualizing the arrangement of the human skeleton. By creating a picture in my mind of linking the bones of my wrist to my arms, to my spine, to my hips, to my legs, and to the ground, I am able to create a continuous, flexible pathway from the hand to the ground. Eventually this visual image becomes a physical reality. When my partner pushes on my wrist, I do not stop his power with the muscles in my forearm or shoulder, but allow the power to flow from bone to bone, like links in a chain, until it runs into the ground. The earth then absorbs my partner's power and I am unaffected by it.

Alignment can also be described as a drainage pipe channeling water. The pipe must have no sharp bends to impede or block the water's flow. If there are, the water will stop flowing smoothly and most likely, the pipe's walls would burst. Instead, the pipe channels the water effortlessly and directs it someplace. In the case of the defender, his body acts like the pipe and the attacker's power flows easily into the ground.

Question: Does the size of the attacker make any difference?

Answer: No. Training partners may be big, but the earth has an infinite mass in comparison. By aligning my skeletal structure with the path of my partner's power and directing it into the ground, I allow the earth's mass to receive it.

When attacked, I recommend that students start using one of the visualizations of alignment described earlier, and directing the power of their attacker through their center, into the ground, and back again to apply a technique. The sequence is: attacker-hand-center-ground-center-hand-attacker-throwing technique.

Finally, while the student physically aligns his or her body and skeletal structure, he or she aligns mentally. Whether by using visualization or by focusing one's intent, the student's thinking must be in accord with his or her body.

Question: What are you thinking when you become aligned and are using ground strength?

Answer: First, my awareness is focused on my hands, arms, shoulders, back, hips, and legs working together in the same direction, so that my body is unified. This is the full body awareness I mentioned earlier.[14]

Second, I focus on maintaining good balance. Standing balance, that is standing alone by myself, is a different kind of balance than when I am practicing with a partner. Standing alone, it is easy to keep from falling down, but if my partner gives a little push, it requires a different kind of balance. I must adjust my feet and create a wider stance so that my partner's force automatically goes into the ground via my center and my legs.

Each situation is different, but somehow I must work to make a balance that is as nearly perfect as possible. This kind of training is what I call developing centeredness.

Question: You have described the general view of the relationship of the upper body to the lower body. Would you describe what the individual parts of the human body do in working together as a unit?

Answer: Beginning with my head, where I look is very important. I line up my eyes and my nose with my navel. Wherever the navel is pointing, that is where I am looking. My arms are relaxed and at my sides. With the human body, this is the most natural position for strength and power.

If your face is turned away, even a little bit, then your awareness and focus are turned away too. This makes your balance weaker and you will lose some of your power. One application of this concept is to turn your partner's face away when you are throwing her, which makes her less powerful and easier to throw.

Question: In that regard what do you do with your shoulders in order to maintain your own power?

Answer: The shoulders line up with the rest of the body and the navel; however, there is a bit of a variation, because the shoulders also align with the legs. With basic movement, if the right leg is forward, the right shoulder should also be a little bit forward. This helps with balance.

Equally important as the shoulder-leg alignment is the position of the shoulders. Shoulders should be in a natural position, rotated neither forward nor back, and held straight across. If the shoulders lift up, this position lessens power and reduces balance. By keeping the shoulders down, this will help to concentrate awareness and focus in the *seika tanden.*

Another way to say this is that if you want to make your partner weaker, then raise his shoulders, but if you want to have more strength to throw him, keep your shoulders down.

Question: A lot of people have one arm dangling unused at their side when they receive an attack. How does this position affect their alignment?

Answer: Using just one arm means that only part of your body is aligned instead of all of it. Most people who assume this position, do it as part of a practice habit. Because they are engaging in movement practice in the dojo and their partners are moving for them, they can get away with it. It is up to them to correct this habit and use both arms when receiving an attack.

You should always have your hands in front of your solar plexus. This placement is natural for concentrating your power through your alignment. If one hand is behind your back, then your power is reduced.

For example, stand with your right foot forward and your right hand held forward at chest height, arm extended and slightly bent. Then place your left hand behind your back. Have a partner push on your hand. Your partner will easily push you backward. Now bring your left hand forward to your side. This time when your partner pushes, it will be more difficult for him to move you. Finally, bring your left hand all the way forward and even with your right. When your partner pushes you in this position, he will hardly be able to move you at all.

If you want to access the power that alignment develops, then you must bring your hands to the front, otherwise you are using only one arm. Moreover, with both hands in front of you, you create several triangles between your arms, your body, and the ground. One triangle is formed by the two arms themselves. Two more are formed through each arm and leg to the ground. Finally, there is an overall pyramid shape created by the body, the arms, and the ground.

The triangle is an extremely powerful geometric figure. It helps concentrate your focus and balance. If you take one arm away, then the triangles disappear and that makes you weaker.

Of course, some people are naturally strong in their upper body and the loss of power is not so apparent. Even so, if they bring both arms to the front, they will become more balanced and more powerful with less effort. For the average person, on the other hand, it is always better if the arms are held in front. When she turns her body, say during *tenkan,* her arms and hands should always be in front of her solar plexus. In this manner, she can maintain power while turning.

Later on, a student depends on training to develop this alignment so that it can be extended outside the body and still maintain power. For example, O Sensei could perform a staff demonstration with many attackers pushing on the end of the staff and it did not move. It was his practice to extend his alignment from his arms to the tip of the staff.

Question: How do the hands and the fingers relate to the rest of the body?

Answer: If the hand and the fingers are tight then the elbow will be tight. This means the shoulder will be tight and as a result the entire body cannot function properly. By this I mean that when the muscles are tense, alignment is disrupted at the point of tension. Therefore, it is very important to maintain the fingers and hands in a relaxed state. It sounds very simple, but sometimes the simplest ideas are the most difficult to implement.

Defender grabs the attacker's forearm with both hands. Both elbows are pointed upward and out to the side. In this position she is very weak and the attacker is able to knock her to the side.

Defender received the attack with his forearms. Both elbows are down and the attack is neutralized.

For example, Aikido beginners often receive a *shomenuchi*[15] attack by trying to grab their partner's forearm and elbow with their hands. Receiving a *shomenuchi* strike in this manner only works if your partner is doing the movement for you. However, if someone attacks strongly, at worst this attack could break the thumbs and maybe even the hand; at best, you will be using only the power of your arm and will be easily overwhelmed.

Question: In aligning the upper body we make certain the head, shoulders and chest are lined up with the navel. What is the proper alignment for the lower half of the body?

Answer: The lower half of the body supports the upper half and completes the link to ground. The knees must stay relaxed and be slightly flexed. This way you can rotate 360 degrees easily. If your knees are tense, you will move sluggishly and be unable to make a solid connection with the ground.

The ankles are the joints that connect the feet with the upper body. They must stay flexible and relaxed in order to maintain balance and to channel the power from the ground to the arms, and vice versa.

With the body properly aligned, the arms, shoulders, back, hips, and legs are integrated into a single powerful unit. In this state you can easily channel your partner's attack through your *seika tanden* into the ground. When this alignment is effective, you are able to use the attacker's power to increase your balance while at the same time breaking his balance without resorting to muscle power. Moreover, it helps establish the connection between your *seika tanden* and your partner's *seika tanden* so that wherever you move, he moves.[16]

Question: Is it possible that I will only have to use ten percent of my power if I have my body properly aligned and integrated?

Answer: Yes.

Question: So far you've described alignment during training sessions. How do you maintain alignment when the attack is not so predictable?

Answer: Maintaining alignment goes back to a pre-contact connection with the attacker. When your body and mind are aligned, you automatically move to connect with your attacker so that his attack is neutralized. In other words, you can automatically move where the technique can happen.

Question: How do I maintain my alignment in order to apply the right technique when somebody is grabbing onto my wrist or punching me?

Answer: Another way to look at this is to observe a great basketball player, like Michael Jordan. I've noticed that he is the most relaxed player on the court. I believe it goes back to what I said about relaxation. His body and mind work together and he automatically knows to shoot or pass, or whatever is needed at that moment.

Eventually, by moving in alignment and connection with our Aikido partners, we automatically know what technique is needed because we are in the right place for that technique to happen.

In other words, I am moving and find a technique that is already there. I don't have to make it happen. I would not not say that I am creating that technique, but that when I move, that technique is already there. It is as if there is nothing else to do at that moment. You create a relationship with your partner by connecting with him or her and then the technique emerges from that relationship.

Question: That seems to be the opposite of the way we practice.

Answer: Beginners practice repetitively at first because they are concentrating on learning the movements and the techniques, and not on creating the relationship. But as they learn about alignment and center-to-center connection, the sequence of learning reverses to form the relationship first. After many years of practice, alignment determines movement, not the other way around.

Question: What are some exercises to practice alignment?

Answer: Begin with awareness. Every day, every practice, think about your body's alignment from the ground to your partner, using your visualizations. Second, check what you are thinking when you practice. If you are fighting with your partner, chances are that you are only using your arms or shoulders. That tendency arises from a desire to throw your partner down instead of focusing on alignment.

As your mind gives up the desire to fight and win, work on your connection with your partner and establishing the center-to-center connection between your *seika tanden* and your partner's *seika tanden*. Then you can use one of the neutralization methods presented in the second part of the book to break his balance. At this point the application of technique follows.

Two exercises, *funakoki undo* and *ikkyo-undo* are excellent beginning practices. These exercises require you to focus straight ahead on an imaginary target or opponent. You must be in a natural posture—one foot forward and the other back, with knees slightly bent, your shoulders low and relaxed, and both arms must be ready to move in unison. Then with the feet stationary, shift your hips forward and backward. The arms move with the motion of the body, swinging naturally. The value of the training is in maintaining alignment of all body parts during this movement .

Question: What is the best way to develop the ability to align with your opponent?

Answer: There are many exercises to develop alignment, but perhaps the easiest way to acquire an understanding of how alignment works is to push a car around a parking lot. Though flippant sounding, this practice instructs the body in proper alignment by employing a physical impediment to a simple movement. If your legs are not lined up properly with your arms, shoulders, and torso, you will be unable to move the car at all.

You can also do this practice in the dojo by pushing a partner across the mat. Focus on your alignment, using your legs and ground connection, as you push him. Then have your partner push you. This time direct his power through your body into the mat so that he is pushing against the Earth. Once you have established the feeling for alignment apply it to all your techniques.

There is no secret to this. Learning connection/alignment, or position/timing, or centeredness/balance requires focusing your awareness on these aspects of Aikido during practice. Of course, it is impossible to concentrate on all of these Second Level Training concepts at once. So you must focus on them individually, perhaps working on connection/alignment one month, and then position/timing one month, and so on and so on. In this manner all of them grow separately, until they begin to coalesce in your practice.

Chapter 5

CONNECTION

Second Level Training works on creating an ability to form a power connection with your partner or attacker at that moment of what we call "first touch." A third level of training establishes another kind of connection between you and your partner, a yoking of movement that can occur before first touch. In fact, this yoking of movement must happen during an encounter with an attacker, although it is not the primary subject of this book. Second Level Training develops the skill that enables you to feel the direction and intent of your partner's attack when you physically contact

him by linking your physical center, your seika tanden, *with his by forming this power connection. One way to look at this center-to-center connection is as a power line that joins two people from* seika tanden *to* seika tanden. *Establishing this kind of connection through the power line is what enables you to unbalance an attacker.*

The defender fails to make the center-to-center connection applying force in the direction of his pointed finger which is away from the attacker.

· 53 ·

The defender makes the center-to-center connection, unbalancing his attacker, as demonstrated by where his finger is pointing.

You can use this power line to determine the direction and intent of an attack without losing your own balance or otherwise putting your body at risk of injury. Moreover, by using this connection, a defender is able to break his attacker's balance and more easily move his attacker in the same motion as he moves himself. For many years now in her Aikido seminars, Mary Heiny Sensei has taught the value of this center-to-center connection. Relating it to her own ability to throw partners much larger than herself, she commented, "With this connection, you can let it go so they [partners] fall into a hole."

Making the power connection between you and your attacker is the most important aspect of SLT. Once this connection is consistently and easily made, the whole dynamic of dealing with attacks and creating joint locks and throws gradually changes. The focus of training evolves from throwing a person as a separate entity to neutralizing his power and then moving as one.

Question: What is meant by making a connection with your partner?

Answer: This kind of connection is a physical connection between two or more people. Whether grabbing the wrist with one hand or two hands, or whether it is a strike or a punch, there is always a physical connection between you and your partner. However, connection is not just a situation in which you have been grabbed or hit, but is a result of the contact. You connect your *seika tanden* to your partner's *seika tanden* and actually establish a tactile connection that you feel in your physical center.[17]

Question: How do you create this connection from *seika tanden* to *seika tanden*?

Answer: It begins when my partner touches me. The moment of contact is the beginning of a power line from my *seika tanden* to my partner's, enabling me to channel the force, intent, and direction of his attack into my *seika tanden* through whatever part of my body he grabs or strikes— the wrist, shoulder, forearm, etc. By pushing back a little bit, I can establish a direct power connection to my partner's *seika tanden* and at this moment in the attack center-to center-connection is initiated.

If my partner pushes, then this push creates power and I can feel it and I can connect with it. But if my partner is lazy and does not push, then I have to push to make power. In some way there has to be power— pushing, pulling or striking—and that power creates connection.

Also, in order to establish this center-to-center connection successfully, I must move slightly forward to engage the attacker before he makes contact. If I wait, then the attacker will establish control of the center-to-center connection. Finally, I must maintain internal alignment, centeredness, whole-body movement, and remain relaxed.

Question: Does it matter where your partner grabs or where he strikes you?

Answer: No. You can establish a center-to-center connection from any attack. Whether it is a grab to the wrist, forearm, leg, or torso, or a strike to the body or the head, the essence of center-to-center connection is that I establish a powerline connection with my attacker so that I feel the direction of his attack as though I were joined directly with his *seika tanden.*

Defender can find the center and unbalance her attacker from any attack when she touches the attacker's body through his wrist, forearm, or shoulder.

The attacker grasps the defender's wrist.

The attacker grasps the defender's elbow.

The attacker grasps the defender's shoulder.

However, with wrist grabs or shoulder grabs, it is easy to demonstrate that power makes a connection. We can more readily feel our partner's power as he or she pushes or pulls us. This connection is very immediate and, comparatively speaking, lasts a long time. But there is also a connection with strikes. A strike does not have the same connection as grabbing, like two railroad cars coupling. It is more immediate and visceral—a shock to the entire body. And that is the key. Whether a partner attacks with a grab or a strike, it is still a body-to-body connection and therefore a center-to-center connection can be established.

If my partner attacks with a stick to the side of my head, for example, I have to move either forward or backward to reduce the power of the attack to less than 100 percent. Then I can connect with his power. Connecting with my partner's power, I can feel his strength and its direction in my body and therefore blend with it if I want to.

Sometimes the center connection alone is enough to handle an attacker who is unskilled and is not attacking my center with a grab or a strike.

Question: What happens if the attacker is a skilled martial artist who attempts to connect to your center with his attack?

Answer: When this happens, your partner can catch your center or you can catch her center. This position appears to be a stalemate, but the defender can break out of it by using one of the neutralization methods described in the second section of this book. Some of these methods can be accomplished from a static connection and others have to be achieved through timing and position so that at the instant the center connection is made, your partner's power is greatly reduced.

Question: Is there any sensation before this physical connection is established?

Answer: Ancient warriors said that they could already feel the enemy attack before an assault. In some ways, this type of intuition was the result of living in a paranoid world where anyone could be a friend or an enemy. If you did not develop a sixth sense, your chances of survival were slim. In our own century, O Sensei said that during the Russian-Japanese War of 1905, he could feel the intent and direction of the Russian soldiers firing their weapons before they actually pulled the triggers. Of course, this was during war time, but we can develop the same skills today to assist us in our martial arts training. When we walk into a room we can see people who are angry, and knowing this we can act appropriately. One does not have to be paranoid to spot an angry person or a group of young thugs.

Remember the simple fact that in a fight it is impossible for an attacker to hurt you unless there is actual physical contact. Even a weapon must strike you. The sensational action-at-a-distance phenomena sometimes expressed in the martial arts are fantasies best left to the cinema.

Question: How does this awareness change when an an angry person or a thug begins an attack?

Answer: You have to set up the proper position and exercise the proper timing so that when the opponent touches you, you make his body a part of your body.

Question: For some people, the appearance of the attacker, especially if he is large or frightening, is unnerving. When they are attacked, they are unable to move to the right place or make any kind of connection. The result is that they get beaten. Is there some secret to learning how to make this *seika tanden* connection under stress?

Answer: There is no secret to this, it is simply practice and experience. You have to have the knowledge that you can execute the movement, timing, and connection. In order to acquire this knowledge, you have to practice many different ways—movement practice, hard training, soft training, training with different-sized people—so that you have a wide and deep foundation of experience to draw on. Once you have acquired this experience, you can relax, and being relaxed means that you can survive any kind of attack. If you practice enough, then you can move properly and deal with any situation.

Question: Are there any connection exercises students can practice?

Answer: Tenkan and *irimi* are very important exercises for learning the power line connection. When your partner grabs your wrist during these exercises, focus on feeling the direction and the intent of your partner's attack. From there proceed to establishing a connection from your *seika tanden* to your partner's *seika tanden*. Take the time to be aware that your body and your partner's body are joined. Then when you move, practice moving your partner as a part of your body. You have to use your mind to direct your attention to become aware of what is happening during these three steps. You have to use your awareness to practice them.

In Aikido and in other martial arts, we often only work on the movements that form techniques and kata. This builds a foundation that is only a foundation for the movements, not for handling realistic attacks. I am not denigrating these martial skills, however, if you want to continue to develop, a shift in training must occur. I am not saying that what I am offering is the only answer, but it has worked for many students. What I have found is that the power connection derived from full body awareness, body alignment, and centeredness leads to the possibility of directly neutralizing the power of the attack in some simple and direct ways.

One of the most interesting aspects of the power connection is that the greater the connection the less the pressure that is needed to control or throw an attacker. It is as if the power connection is some fundamental principle of control.

Section Two

THE APPLICATIONS OF POWER

Building on the center-to-center power connection developed in Section One, Section Two of this book is devoted to four means of neutralizing attackers. These four methods are different in appearance and execution, but are derived from the same principle—breaking down an attacker's balance so that any attempt at aggressive action is reduced or ineffectual.

The principle at play here is disrupting a person's power as a result of upsetting a delicate balance, which is not inherent in the mass and shape of the body, but which must be actively maintained. Consider a 200-pound statue in the form of a human. Even at its most stable, for a person half its weight it is easy to tip it over. The statue's mass cannot maintain its balance when pushed and cannot be employed in delivering power for an attack.

Section Two of this book explores how to make a living opponent as unstable as that statue and then take advantage of this instability to effect a technique, throw, or strike.

In Section One we addressed methods for increasing our balance. When this balance is developed in relation to an attacking force, it is called centeredness. We learned that through centeredness the force of an opponent's attack actually increases the defender's balance, making the attack a positive rather than a negative development. We then explored how relaxation and proper body alignment are the two key components to expanding centeredness.

In addition, we saw that the easiest way to effect control over an attacker is through a center-to-center power connection. We know that if we connect to a person's center, we can affect his or her whole mind/body relationship. Any disruption in an opponent's balance automatically induces a weakened state. Moreover, only by great force of will can an attacker avoid attempting to regain his lost balance once it is disrupted. The requisite effort to restore balance diminishes the power of the attack up to the point of its total abandonment.

However, in the last chapter of Section One we began to see that the center-to-center power connection may not be enough to handle a skilled martial artist. First, a skilled martial artist may use the center-to-center power connection to control the defender's center, rendering the defender off balance and weaker. Second, even if a defender has good centeredness and forms a positive center-to-center power connection, control can be lost when he or she applies a technique or takes some other martial action. A defender must make his opponent weaker than he or she is. Even if the opponent is bigger, stronger, or faster, there is some means, through grounding, uprooting, spiraling, or timing and position, to make the opponent weak.

To augment the elements of power discussed in Section One and make them useful in fighting situations, neutralization techniques are explained in Section Two. These neutralization methods nullify an opponent's advantages in speed, strength, and size. In the following chapters we can learn how to apply the methods of neutralization at the moment of center-to-center power connection.

Briefly, the first two methods of neutralization—grounding and uprooting—can be practiced from static attacks and are, therefore, more basic in that they allow for a more ideal learning opportunity. They also have a wider range of applications; for example, grounding can be useful in all fighting situations, including grappling. Grounding employs the natural tendency of any person to stay rooted to the earth for balance and control by increasing the person's weight and making mobility difficult or even impossible. Uprooting, on the other hand, lifts an opponent from his naturally grounded state to a position of weightless ineffectualness, therefore making him easy to move.

Spiraling is the third neutralization techniques and is employed after grounding and uprooting to further reduce an opponent's ability to regain *his balance and continue attacking by turning his attack away from its intended impact point.*

Lastly, timing and position are not themselves neutralization techniques, but in Aikido, timing and position involve moving to the proper place appropriate to your opponent's intent and attack in order to establish a center-to-center relationship. In this manner they become a means of arriving at a neutralization technique at the moment of first touch. Timing and position require movement before first touch and place a defender where an opponent's attack is least compelling and forceful. The subtlety of moving in accord with an opponent so that her full power is not effective makes this method more difficult to learn.

Chapter 6

GROUNDING

For most people, the ability to deliver a powerful attack or to resist a grappling technique is largely a function of "balance." Balance consists of the body's alignment in relation to the ground and the freedom to perform center movements, as evidenced by weight shifts. Without balance, attacks are at best inadequately executed. There are, of course, many other reasons why an attack may fail, for example, poor aim or weak intention.

However, the reason balance is such an important focus of Second Level Training is that Aikido deals with an attack by leading an attacker, after first touch, through one of a series of techniques that results in either a pin or a throw without injuring the attacker. In order for a defender to perform an Aikido technique successfully against an aggressive, powerful attacker, the defender must dissipate the attacker's power, in a martial sense, over a long period of time during the course of the attack. If the goal of Aikido were to render the opponent unconscious, the focus of the training would be undoubtedly different. But Aikido requires control of the attacker's center, his balance, from the beginning to the end of the technique, which results in a safe resolution of the conflict for both attacker and defender. One of the most effective ways to gain this control is to form the center-to-center power connection and then neutralize the attacker's power through grounding.

Grounding means driving your partner's weight into the earth and restricting his freedom of movement. Grounding can be likened to being caught in a room where the ceiling is collapsing. In order to make it to the door to escape, you must hold the ceiling above your head with your arms extended and walk through the debris-filled room. Under the continuous tension caused by the weight of the ceiling, not only do you become tired quickly, but your movements are sluggish and powerless. If required to move constantly under this type of stress, you soon collapse.

Our own experience training with different Aikido teachers has shown us that those who employ grounding are able to disrupt an attacker's quickness and movement, weakening him. Other students who have experienced this comment afterwards that they felt "buried in the mat" and "the strain involved in trying to move exhausted me completely." Such comments underscore the efficacy of grounding as a neutralization technique and create the impression that martial artists who use this technique seem to have discovered a way to make themselves heavier than normal during training. We believe this explanation is not quite accurate. For example, what we believe is that these teachers force their attackers to push against the ground connection while in a compromised position. To continue our metaphor, the attackers are pushing against the ceiling and cannot let go for fear of the roof collapsing.

Question: Please explain the concept of breaking balance.

Answer: The Japanese have a character for breaking balance—*kuzushi*, "causing an object to change from a stable situation to an unstable one; or to disturb the integrity of an object's structure."[18] *Kuzushi* means to affect your partner's centeredness so that she becomes unbalanced and weak. This state allows you to move your partner no matter what the size and strength differences.

Question: How is *kuzushi* created?

Answer: There are many methods of employing *kuzushi*. We could use the terms, "uprooting," "grounding," and "spiraling" in order to describe their physical effects. Also, "timing and position" is another element that is involved in breaking balance. The second section of this book examines each one separately, but actually, they are all parts of the same whole and are often used together in one technique.

Question: With the idea of *kuzushi* in mind, would you please explain what you mean by grounding your partner?

At a seminar in Boulder, April 1999, Frank Doran Sensei demonstrated grounding by using Aikido's ikkyo *movement from cross hand grab.*[19] *As his partner grasped Doran's right wrist, Sensei moved forward and down, dropping his center closer to the mat, causing the opponent to stagger. He was unable to move as his body was driven into the ground and a bit to one side, making him lose his balance. From this position, the more the partner pushed against Sensei, the more unbalanced he became. Since the Earth has an infinite mass compared to the human body, the attacker was unable to push it away. As Doran Sensei continued the grounding neutralization technique, the partner's knees buckled and he fell to the mat.*

Defender receives a two-hand grab.

The defender makes the center-to-center connection, immediately unbalancing the attacker.

The defender grounds the attacker by shifting his weight to the outside of his right foot.

Close up perspective showing the attacker's weight on the outside of his right foot.

Answer: In this neutralization technique, after I establish center-to-center connection, I visualize connecting through my partner's center and compressing his body into the ground so that as he pushes back at me the direction of his effort is routed in such a manner that he is compelled to push against the ground beneath my feet and is therefore unable to move his legs effectively.

After sliding beside the attacker's strike to avoid a blow to the solar plexus, the defender makes a center-to-center connection, grounding him through the striking arm and causing his legs to buckle.

Another way to explain this is to say that for most human beings the greatest power lies in their legs. So when I am grounding my attacker, I am restricting my opponent's leg power while keeping my mobility fluid.

The defender makes the center-to-center connection, immediately unbalancing the attacker.

Question: When an opponent grasps your wrist with a one-hand grab, he's on both feet and aligned to the ground; he's centered and balanced. What do you do to compromise his balance as he grabs your wrist?

Answer: First, I am connected to the ground, I am well-balanced. My body is aligned internally and I am connected to my partner. In addition, my body is structurally integrated so that I do not respond to the attack with isolated muscles groups. As my partner grasps my wrist I make a center-to-center connection. Then my body leans through him as though I am doing *funakoki undo* or the rowing exercise.[20] I shift my weight and his weight into one of his feet or both feet and a little bit to the outside or the inside, depending upon where I want to go. As I explained before, he is now forced to push against the ground beneath my feet.

Now my partner's power is vastly reduced. What little power he has, he is using to try and stop himself from falling down. Moreover, his attention is directed toward his feet and the tension in his body is directed downward through my feet, increasing my balance and making me stronger. He can no longer use his legs to move around, or to create power, or to channel ground strength. On the other hand, I still have my balance, mobility, connection and alignment, and I can use the power in my legs and the ground. Now that my partner is in a weakened state and I have established the center-to-center connection, wherever I move my center his center follows. This is done with no more effort than if he were not there.

Question: Where is your power coming from?

Answer: From my legs and pushing against the ground, but, in addition, my entire body is working as an integrated unit. If my whole body does not work together, then the power from the ground and my legs will be blocked at my hips, or back, or shoulders and I will be unable to affect my partner and ground him.

Grounding, as well as all neutralization techniques, relies on my body acting in an integrated fashion in order to succeed.

Question: How much time do you have to accomplish grounding?

Answer: The amount of time it takes to exploit this power varies depending upon experience. More experienced people can ground their partners more quickly. In the early stages of learning this neutralization technique, it may take you seconds to find it and learn to apply it. After you practice it for a while, the goal becomes to apply it at first touch so that no time elapses at all between the opponent's attack and inducing his weakened state.

Question: Let's go back to Aikido training. How important is grounding in day-to-day technique?

Answer: It is very important. Grounding stops the attacker's movement, takes away the attacker's strength, and it creates that fraction of time necessary to apply a technique. In a fighting situation, technique is almost impossible without grounding or some form of neutralization. Otherwise, the contest goes to the biggest, the most powerful, and the swiftest. So you need to practice these neutralization methods daily if you want to succeed at Second Level Training.

Question: What do we have to do to be successful in applying a neutralization technique like grounding?

Answer: As I explained earlier in Section One, when we were discussing Second Level Training, you must develop centeredness. Centeredness provides the balance you need to handle an attacker. This type of balance allows your movements to be fluid and free, and still be powerful in relation to the attacker because of your alignment and connection to the earth.

Question: You would think that being driven into the ground would be an advantage.

Answer: It would be if I were driving my opponent straight into the ground through his own legs and making him more balanced and powerful, but I am not. At first, I am merely forming a center-to-center connection. Then, using the *funakoki undo* movement, I put everything into one or the other of my opponent's legs and direct it to the outside or inside. That way I can break the attacker's balance, making him weaker.

When my opponent first attacks me in the grounded state, I automatically channel his power straight into the ground through my legs, augmenting my own balance. When this power is rebounded to my attacker, I direct the power to one side or the other so he loses his balance. In other words, the attacker's groundedness moves to one side or the other through one leg or sometimes both legs, disrupting his alignment and ground connection and disturbing his balance.

Question: How do you direct this grounding technique from one side to the other in order to make the opponent lose balance?

Answer: I can include a twisting motion toward the ground—a kind of corkscrewing motion—which helps to break the opponent's balance. This twisting motion, which comes from the third neutralization technique spiraling, makes the legs buckle and drives them into the ground. In this manner, grounding and spiraling work together to weaken an opponent by making him unbalanced.[21]

Question: Can you employ grounding at any time, say after the opponent has grabbed you?

Answer: If you try to ground a skilled opponent after he has attacked, when his balance and strength are at 100 percent and he has established good alignment and connection to the ground, then this neutralization technique is more difficult to apply. Your opponent already has the initiative, and with his speed and strength he may be able to overpower you. Therefore, you must make the skilled opponent weak before he attacks or at the moment of first touch when you have established the center-to-center connection.

Of course, if the attack is uncommitted or unskilled it is not much of a problem to neutralize the opponent through grounding. Remember, these kind of skills are always relational, based on the skill and intent of your partner.

Question: Would you give us a simple grounding practice?

Answer: During training, have your partner grab your wrist and push forward establishing the center-to-center connection. Relax your arm so that you can channel the force of your partner's attack through your legs and into the ground beneath your feet. If you need to, place your elbow against your hip so that you can channel your partner's attack more directly through your hips and down your legs into the ground. Then take the time to feel the direction and intent of your partner's attack clearly. Next, push back with your whole body, using the rowing motion while at the same time directing your weight in a movement blending forward and downward motions through your partner's body and into the ground. This type of practice is the basic method to learn to apply the grounding technique.

However, at some time during the course of their training, beginners must learn that martial arts practice and actual fighting are distinct. In fighting, an opponent grabs and punches at the same time. So the grounding movement has to be simultaneous with or immediately follow the point of connection. Anything less and we could die.

In Aikido, basic training usually deals with one attack at a time and the rules are such that training partners are either on defense or offense, but not both at the same time. If your primary martial art is Aikido, in order to explore some of these concepts more deeply, you may have to vary your daily training by occasionally eliminating the distinction in roles and types of attacks.

Question: In a fighting situation, balance and ground connection must exist all the time. Without them we would be overpowered. Is this true?

Answer: Yes, I must be ready to receive an opponent's power all the time. If I do not have balance throughout the fighting process, I cannot possibly throw my attacker and will probably be knocked down myself.

However, if my balance is right, I can break my opponent's balance through a neutralization technique like grounding.

Question: How do you stay balanced?

Answer: Balance while training or fighting is fluid, since our bodies are always adjusting to our opponent's movements as well as our own. Some of the physical things to focus on are adjusting the feet and body, as well as slightly bending the knees in order to stay aligned and connected to the ground.

Question: Sometimes in practice when students perform a technique on their partners, the partners turn it around effortlessly. How does that happen?

Answer: This could be because of grounding. Let us use, for example, the Aikido technique called *sankyo*.

When you apply sankyo on me, if I receive it with my shoulder in the air and my elbow pointing toward the ceiling, you can throw me easily, I am on my tip toes and my mobility is compromised.

But when I drop my shoulders and align my body so that my weight is directed through your legs and I am grounding you, this not only stops your movement, but takes away your balance. This means I have the freedom of movement I need to reverse the technique.

The attacker applies sankyo to the defender, lifting his shoulder and elbow into the air.

Defender makes the center-to-center con- nection by pushing in toward the attacker while at the same time dropping his elbow and shoulder and driving the force of the attack onto the attacker's right foot.

The defender now has the attacker under his control for either a throw or a strike.

Once a person is grounded, it is easy for the defender to move his or her feet. By constantly adjusting the ground connection, one achieves a great deal of control over the attacker while still being free to move.

Grounding so restricts freedom of movement that the opponent loses much of his power. So in a broad sense, this loss of freedom means being weak.

Chapter 7

UPROOTING

If grounding drives an opponent's body into the earth so that his freedom of movement is impaired, uprooting is the opposite of grounding: lifting an opponent out of the well of gravity and converting his mobility into unco-ordinated ineffectualness. Many of us do not employ uprooting effectively, but instead haphazardly push our opponents, hoping they will somehow magically lose their balance in the process. Through uprooting you con-sciously direct the force of your opponent's attack upward and outward, reducing her ground connection—and therefore her power—and destroy-ing her balance. Once this has been accomplished, the defender can easily move his opponent as long as he maintains the center-to-center power line.

Question: Could you describe the mechanics of the basic uprooting movement in response to a wrist grab?

Answer: I align my opponent's arm with my arm so that I can make a straight-line connection to his shoulder. In a one-hand grab, it is also important that the bones of my wrist extend directly through the web of skin between my opponent's thumb and forefinger. This technical detail helps not only to keep the two arms straight but to make a direct con-nection from my body up through my opponent's arm bones to his shoulder. Then I shift my center forward in order to lift his shoulder, causing his weight to move upward and weakening his balance. Finally, I add a little twist that rotates his shoulder forward, further uprooting him and reducing his power.

The attacker grasps the defender's wrist.

The defender pushes back, making a center-to-center connection with his attacker.

The direction of defender's push is up the attacker's arm to the point of her shoulder and raising her shoulder to her ear. He adds a little arm twist to augment the uprooting motion of the attacker's shoulder.

The defender slides forward, further uprooting the attacker and disrupting her balance.

Close up of the attacker's feet showing that she is off balance and dependent upon the defender for her own balance.

Question: What does the twisting do?

Answer: A part of the center-to-center connection, twisting enables me not only to pick up his shoulder but lift up my opponent's entire body, breaking his connection with the ground. After that I can apply a technique.

Question: So your initial movement is to create center-to-center connection?

Answer: Yes. As I explained in Section One, I have to feel my opponent's power coming into me. Then, once I have established center-to-center connection, I must connect my arm and my opponent's arm in a straight line to the shoulder in order to raise his shoulder and break his balance.

However, it is most important that the center-to-center connection does not end once I have lined up the arms. At this moment, my arm has to move forward at the same time my center does, like executing *funakoki undo*, so that I am not only extending my hand. Otherwise, I will lose the center-to-center connection and my power, and will be unable to implement the twist that helps raise the shoulder.

Beginning students who have not yet learned the Second Level Training discussed in Section One often thrust their hands forward first without using their bodies. This is the reason their opponents are able to break their balance and make them weaker, disrupting the flow of their technique. In order to uproot your opponent properly, your hand and body must move together with full-body integration, as discussed in Section One.[22]

Question: What if you don't have any balance? Can you then uproot an opponent?

Answer: It would be highly unlikely, unless your opponent was very accommodating and moved for you. In order to make uprooting, or any of the neutralizing methods work, there are three things you must establish.

First, you must establish your own centeredness so that you are connected to the ground and you have balance. This kind of centeredness is a living, moving state of being. Without it, you are like the 200 pound statue and are easily uprooted and knocked over by an opponent's attack.

Second, your body must be integrated and your alignment established from your hand to your feet. This complements your centeredness and gives you whole body power when moving.

Finally, you must initiate center-to-center connection. If any one of these three steps is missing, then you will be unable to implement uprooting successfully.

Question: Does it matter if the attacker is lined up properly in order for you to uproot him or her successfully?

Answer: In a fighting situation, no opponent is willingly going to line up his or her arm with your arm. It is your job to accomplish this type of alignment. Only when beginners are first learning about uprooting do senior partners help them by lining up for them.

Question: What happens to an opponent when he is uprooted?

Answer: Most often you initially see his shoulder or shoulders lift up. Then his center skews to one side or the other. As his balance is broken, he begins to lose his alignment with the ground and he feels lighter so that it becomes easier to move him around. This last part is very interesting, since an opponent's weight seems to diminish when he has been uprooted. Clearly, he still weighs the same, however, part of his weight is now involved with falling, which makes his body easier to move.

Another way to look at this concept is that when an opponent is uprooted, a portion of his inertia or mass has been converted to kinetic energy by the falling process. In actuality, if at any moment we were to freeze the action, the opponent's total weight that is directed toward the ground would be the same as before he was uprooted.

Question: Is the opponent's weight directed down through you once he is moving?

Answer: It depends on if the opponent is angled toward you or away from you. If he is falling toward you, his weight is transferred through you into the ground. This idea can be demonstrated by placing a 100 pound log on a scale so that it stands straight. Then lean the log toward you. Some of its weight is now resting on you and the indicator shows that less weight is now directed onto the scale.

However, an opponent might be lined up so that his weight is directed away from you. In the example of *musubi*,[23] when you have uprooted your partner so that his elbow is bent upward and away from you, he is falling in the opposite direction and his weight is not being directed through your body into the ground.

The opponent's total weight never changes; it is just that you have realigned his weight so that it no longer goes directly into the ground beneath his feet, adding to his balance and ground connection. Instead, the opponent's weight is angled in a direction that destabilizes his stance and his own weight brings him to the ground.

This concept of weight direction also goes back to the idea that sometimes when you have center-to-center connection with an opponent even though you are the defender, he may be able to throw you just as easily as you throw him because he can shift his weight toward you just as you can shift your weight toward him.

Question: How do you stop the opponent from taking control of the center-to-center connection?

Answer: In this situation, the defender must immediately break the opponent's balance upon receiving her attack, reducing her power. That's why I refer to uprooting, grounding, and the other techniques in Section Two as neutralization techniques. They reduce an opponent's power, restricting her freedom of movement, weakening her so that the defender can more easily apply a technique or a throw.

Saotome Sensei often uses uprooting to reduce an opponent's power. When his wrist is grabbed, Saotome Sensei employs Aikido's blending movement, musubi, *and forces his attacker's elbow and shoulder into the air. The attacker continues moving toward him but can do so with only minimum power and effectiveness.*

Defender employs Aikido's blending movement, musubi, and forces her attacker's elbow and shoulder into the air.

Question: What happens after you have uprooted your opponent?

Answer: The defender continues center-to-center connection, using his whole-body movement to break the opponent's balance even further. When the opponent's power is at its weakest, the defender uses this position to apply a technique or to perform a throw.

Question: How do you maintain the uprooted connection over the course of a movement so that the opponent doesn't simply escape?

Answer: I continue to move with the opponent, maintaining the center-to-center connection, so that he is unable to regain his balance. This idea is similar to walking in a gusting wind; if you keep adjusting your body, then you will not be blown over. If at any time while my opponent and I are connected by the center-to-center power line, I loosen the uprooting technique or allow it to lapse altogether, my opponent will be able to regain his balance.

Question: What's your focus when you are uprooting your partner?

Answer: I am studying my opponent's position to determine whether his stance really warrants uprooting. Perhaps his shoulder and body are so low to the ground that uprooting isn't feasible. In that case, I may have to step back, or turn around, or go forward to disrupt my opponent's balance.

Let me explain it this way. When an opponent attacks, he is trying to move to a position where he can assume proper alignment and ground connection, and fill up his body with balance. In this manner, he will be at his most powerful when he grabs me or strikes me. It may be impossible to use uprooting to neutralize his strength, especially if he is well-grounded and much bigger than I am. In this case I have to change the situation if I wish to apply uprooting. Or it may be that it is impossible to apply uprooting and I have to be prepared to apply a different neutralization technique, such as grounding.

Question: In the previous chapter we discussed grounding. Would you contrast uprooting with grounding?

Answer: Again, the use of grounding or uprooting depends upon the opponent's size and strength, as well as his attack style. If your opponent is bigger and taller than you are, uprooting is sometimes easier than grounding. However, if the opponent is shorter than you are, grounding may be easier. Your size relative to your opponent is also important. If you are taller than he is, uprooting might put you in a position of losing your balance, so grounding would be easier and better for you. The opposite response might apply if the conditions were reversed.

You also have to respond to the opponent's attack, whether it is a grab followed by a punch, or a kick, or a strike of some kind. If you can read your opponent's attack, you can move to a position where you can apply either grounding or uprooting—whichever is most appropriate.

Question: Does weight make a difference in which response to choose?

Answer: Weight is a factor, but the choice depends more upon the opponent's position. For example, if he is pressing down, uprooting is very difficult, but grounding or breaking his balance to one side or the other by spiraling is more easily accomplished.

We have broken the process down into several steps: 1) creating alignment and ground connection; 2) establishing center-to-center partner connection; 3) unbalancing the opponent by using a neutralization technique, such as grounding or uprooting; 4) finally, continuing the neutralization until the opponent is at his weakest and applying a technique. However, the goal of the training is combine all of these steps a single movement.

Question: Can you use uprooting to defend against strikes?

Answer: Yes. The *ikkyo* technique provides an excellent example of uprooting. When the attacker strikes with *shomenuchi,* the defender pushes him upward, uprooting him and upsetting his balance. The defender uses this uprooting movement with a spiral so that her opponent's shoulder is thrust upward and twisted away from her. Uprooting works the same with a *yokomenuchi* strike or a hooking punch to the side of the head.

It is vitally important in defending against a striking attack to move your opponent and take his balance so that he is unable to strike immediately a second time. In dealing with punches to the body, however, grounding is usually easier, since the defender's arm is high-

Uprooting from a shomenucki strike to the forehead or a jab to the face.

Uprooting from yokomenuchi strike.

The defender continues the unbalanced state of the attacker and applies a throw.

With the hook, defender moves forward toward the attacker's shoulder, uprooting him and causing him to lose his balance.

er than the attacker's arm and can move down easily.

Sometimes in order to apply uprooting you have to move to a position that makes uprooting possible. In all striking attacks you are not just dealing with the opponent's hand, but connecting to the opponent's center through his hand, so that you can establish center-to-center connection, then use uprooting or grounding to make him weaker.

When responding to a face punch, beginning students often just grab the attacker's hand or forearm and try to apply a technique. Of course, this kind of response does not work. Uprooting and grounding are not just holding techniques but require pushing with your center while maintaining your body's structural integrity and alignment to the ground. When you perform the movements correctly, you are pushing with your center.

Question: Is there a correlation between the basic types of attacks and the means used to neutralize them?

Answer: Not really. If you move properly, you can apply any neutralization technique to any attack. However, some are more easily used on some attacks because of the nature of the attack. But usually, once you have grounded an opponent, you can reverse the motion and uproot him or her; or if you have uprooted an opponent, you can then ground him or her.

Question: Are there any techniques that you can specifically use to practice grounding or uprooting?

Answer: Tenkan practice is ideally suited to developing grounding, because it is readily apparent when you have impeded your partner's mobility. *Musubi* practice can be used to uproot a partner by lifting his shoulder up before sliding beside him. Whether I am practicing *tenkan* or *musubi,* however, I also want to concentrate on impeding my partner's movement or upsetting his balance.

Chapter 8

SPIRALING

The third neutralization technique is spiraling. Although it employs more sophisticated body mechanics than grounding or uprooting, the successful application of spiraling also depends upon first making the center-to-center connection. Then, like grounding and uprooting, spiraling produces a momentary unbalanced state in the opponent, providing the opening to apply a joint lock, takedown, or throw.

Spiraling involves complex body movements. This may be difficult to visualize in three dimensional space, but it is easily demonstrated. Imagine the body spinning on its vertical axis while descending or rising, combined with bringing the arm toward the body or pushing it away in a winding motion.[24]

As with the other two neutralization techniques discussed in Section Two, spiraling is a combination of ground strength, body alignment and center-to-center connection. By aligning the body to the earth so that ground strength is delivered to the arms through whole-body movement, the defender can impart an immense amount of power through the spinning and winding motions inherent in spiraling. Aligned with ground strength, the winding power of the spiral will redirect an opponent's attack, even to the point of throwing the opponent to the ground or into space.

In Tai Chi Chuan *this spiraling technique is called "reeling silk," (Chan Ssu Jing).[25] Reeling silk is not just a mystical description of power, it is a means to describe the fundamental body strengths that involve "…the winding relationship with* peng *(ground-strength) and connection" which "are considered to be the core strength of Chen-style* Taiji *and* Bagua *and others of the internal martial arts."[26]*

Spiraling has its own pitfalls for the student. Whereas grounding and uprooting movements when demonstrated can appear as though nothing is occurring, spiraling seems to be a distinct and decisive movement that can be shown without a partner. The danger of misapplication is two fold. First, either using or attempting the movement without establishing the center-to-center connection. Second, and perhaps even worse, using only a portion of the complete spiral movement, such as the arm twist, resulting in a loss of body alignment and a severe lessening of one's own power.

Question: Would you describe the different components that go into spiraling.

Answer: As a neutralization technique, spiraling involves three movements. First, the defender must spin on his vertical axis, as though there were a pole sticking through his body from the center of his head and out the groin into the ground. Second, the defender must be able to move either up or down along this vertical axis in a balanced way. Third, the defender's arm exerts a twisting motion while either being brought toward the body or pushed away.

First, defender must spin on her vertical axis.

Secondly, the defender must be able to move either up or down along her vertical axis.

Defender's arm exerts a twisting motion as it drops or extends from the body.

While these separate motions are combined into one movement, the defender must also exercise whole body-movement, maintain consistent body alignment with the earth, extend ground strength to his arms, and establish center-to-center connection with his attacker. If any of these components is missing, then the power of spiraling will be greatly reduced or become completely ineffective.

Sequence depicts the three parts of spiraling combined.

Question: Is it necessary to make a center-to-center connection before employing spiraling?

Answer: Yes. Of course, I can make a spiraling movement without a center-to-center connection. However, unless I have established center-to-center connection with my attacker, I cannot move him with spiraling.

If I don't connect to my attacker's center, although my movement may be very powerful, the attacker can blend with my motion and take my balance. A spiraling defender in and of herself doesn't have any real power, unless, like a whirlwind, she runs into something immobile and overcomes the obstacle simply with her momentum. As I have said many times, center-to-center connection is what makes all of these neutralization techniques effective.

Another way to demonstrate this concept is by using a punch. If an opponent punches at me and I receive his punch by merely twisting my forearm, this action accomplishes very little. The punch is relatively unaffected and will continue forward until it strikes its target.

I have observed students who believe that only a forearm twist is necessary to stop a determined attack. This is not so. The twisting movement by itself will not stop a punch from reaching its target. But if my response is the spiraling movement I described earlier, and if at the same time I connect to my attacker's center, then my opponent's balance will be disrupted and the attack will be weakened severely.

An important point to remember is that I am not pushing my arm down to take my opponent's balance. While my arm twists, my body turns and drops along its vertical axis and my opponent comes with it. Because of the center-to-center connection, he is a part of my body's overall movement.

Question: If you don't use your arms, can you still employ spiraling?

Answer: Yes, as long as I have established the center-to-center connection first.

In order to demonstrate what we mean by this, have a partner grab the shoulder of your gi. Then move forward slightly establishing a center-to-center connection. Turn, bending your knees, and drop your shoulder close to the mat. Your body executes a spiral toward the mat as your knees bend. Connected by his center to your center, your partner loses his balance and falls to the mat.

The defender receives the attack to his shoulder.

The defender moves forward slightly establishing a center-to-center connection with the attacker.

The defender then turns, executing a spiral toward the mat as his knees bend. Connected by his center to his attacker's center, attacker loses her balance and falls to the mat.

Question: How powerful does the spiraling technique have to be?

Answer: The amount of power depends upon the forcefulness of an opponent's attack. If the attack is weak, then the defender needs to generate a lot of internal power. Moreover, the amount of space and time he needs for the spiraling movement is also greater. However, if the attack is strong, then the defender can use the opponent's power against him and the power, space, and time necessary for spiraling are less.

By approaching an attack in this way, I avoid doing too much damage to my opponent and save my strength as well. If my opponent attacks strongly and I respond with equal force, I can do much more damage to his body. Moreover, if I have to continue fighting by engaging more attackers, then I will become tired quickly by using so much of my own power instead of using my opponents' power against them. Sooner or later, as a consequence of using mostly my own power, I will become exhausted. So that is the reason for employing an opponent's power: to protect him or her and to conserve my energy.

Question: Can spiraling be used in conjunction with grounding and uprooting?

Answer: Yes. In fact, while all of these neutralization techniques can be used independently of the others, they are most often more effective if used in conjunction with one another. Really, it depends upon the situation. For example, with a punch to the body, grounding followed by spiraling downward prevents an attacker from being able to strike a second or a third time. His balance is literally spun away during the grounding and spiraling process, making it easier to apply a technique or a throw.

Uprooting can be used with spirals as well. Starting from a deep stance with my knees bent, if a punch is thrown to my face, I turn and move upward along my vertical axis with my arm twisting away from me at the same time. As my arm connects with my opponent's arm, the spiraling motion of my body not only uproots him, but turns his attack away from me, unbalancing him and making him weaker.

The authors use the phrases "breaking balance" and "making weaker" interchangeably. From the defender's point of view, the object of any neutralization technique is "to break an attacker's balance" so as to make it easier to apply a joint lock or enact a throwing technique. From the attacker's point of view, "becoming weaker" is how he or she might describe losing one's balance and being forced either to continue fighting from a powerless position, or to scramble around trying to recover his or her balance and reestablish a stronger position. The attacker may not sense that he or she has been grounded, uprooted, or turned away by a spiraling movement, but he or she does understand suddenly being in a weaker position, unable to respond powerfully.

Question: The motions involved in spiraling must work together all at once, so it helps to know something about what your body is doing. Since many beginners and even advanced martial artists believe they are mimicking the spiral movements you have demonstrated, but in reality are doing something else, how do students execute the spiraling movement properly?

Answer: While all the parts of the body must work together to make spiraling effective, in order to learn this neutralization technique you must be able to isolate and visualize each part. During practice, students must spend some time isolating the relevant parts of the body and executing the necessary motions—bending the knees, turning the hips, and twisting the arms—in order to pattern these movements into the muscles. Then they must practice more by combining them so that they work together seamlessly. Finally, as stated earlier, mindless physical training is not enough. Visualization, such as envisioning your body connected and moving together in one piece, as well as mentally studying these techniques, will make a student stronger.

At first, spiraling movements may feel clumsy and the student may easily lose balance. But through consistent practice and by developing centeredness, the student's movements will stabilize. Eventually, the winding motions necessary to spiraling will become smaller and smaller while delivering even more and more power to neutralize an opponent's attack.

Question: Once you have neutralized an opponent with spiraling, how do you move through to the end of the technique?

Answer: First, you must continue breaking his balance so that his centeredness is gone and he becomes weak. To do this, you maintain the center-to-center connection so that if your center goes down, your opponent goes down. If your center rises, your opponent rises too. In this manner, your body moves through the technique in an integrated fashion with your opponent forced to follow along.

Most importantly, you are not making some exaggerated motion with your hands or arms that is completely irrelevant to the spiraling movement that neutralized your opponent's power in the first place. For example, look at the Aikido technique *ikkyo*. Oftentimes in classes, new students will windmill their arms over their heads trying to perform the *ikkyo* movement demonstrated by their teacher.

By making an uncontrolled movement, the student allows his partner to escape, since he has released his partner's center. If you don't care how your body moves in relation to your partner, she will certainly be able to regain her balance.

The student must first connect with his partner's center, then use a neutralization technique, such as spiraling, to break his partner's balance and make him weak. Finally, while maintaining center-to-center connection, the student must apply the technique with his entire body so that as his center moves, so does his partner, until the partner is forced to assume the proper *ukemi*, or movement, in order to protect himself.

I believe this concept of maintaining center-to-center connection throughout an entire technique can be demonstrated through *kaishiwaza*, or reversing an applied technique. Usually during practice, such as in a *Judo* or *Jujitsu* dojo, when students are practicing the different techniques, attackers protect themselves with the proper *ukemi*. However, sometimes an attacker's centeredness has not been compromised by the defender and he is able to reverse the defender's technique and apply a counter. This reversing movement can only happen if the attacker's centeredness has not been broken initially by the defender or if it does not remain broken during the course of the technique.

Question: Let's return to spiraling in relation to strikes. How does spiraling fit in with punches?

Answer: As with wrist or shoulder grabs, you cannot wait for the opponent to make contact with you. You must disrupt his timing and his balance by stepping forward or to the side. The twisting motion of the arm in combination with the spiraling motion performed by the rest of the body spins the opponent away, oftentimes slamming him into the mat when spiraling is accompanied by grounding. Moreover, because the motion of a strike is inherently very quick, you do not have much time to initiate a large spiraling technique. Therefore, center-to-center connection and spiraling, coupled with a grounding or uprooting movement, must be applied simultaneously in order to neutralize the opponent effectively and prevent another attack. Otherwise, your attacker will keep his centeredness and be able to punch or strike a second time.

Practice should not just consist of a block followed by an attack, or in the case of Aikido, a grab followed by a joint lock or a throw. The moment of touching the opponent should already be the end of the attack. Only in this manner can the opponent be prevented from escaping to attack a second time.

It is important to point out that a spiral exists as an infinite movement in three dimensional space. Another way to put this is, one is always dealing with a piece or section of a spiral.

Chapter 9

TIMING AND POSITION

Any discussion of timing and position is almost certainly doomed to mis-understanding, because timing and position do not simply concern the relationship of objects, but the relationship of objects in motion.

At the highest level of martial awareness, the defender must read the intent of his attacker and move so that when the attack reaches him, the attacker is already unbalanced. However, most of us are unable to step into any fighting situation or even a dojo practice with anything more than a rudimentary ability to read an attacker's intent. Only through practicing timing and position can we acquire any proficiency in divining an attacker's intent.

Because attacks during practice are predictable, students should study timing and position so as to know where to move in order to create that unbalancing effect at the moment of contact. The result is that timing and position can provide the defender an insurmountable advantage when used in conjunction with the neutralization techniques, even when facing a larger and faster opponent.

Question: Students often misunderstand timing as quickness. What does timing mean to you?

Answer: Timing is not just speed. It is a partner-to-partner power relationship. Because a partner has power, we have to move in time and space to the position where our partner's power can be used to our advantage

Question: In terms of mass and speed, if defender and attacker are about the same size, how can timing work to the defender's advantage?

Answer: I do not wait for my opponent to complete his attack. Instead, I change my position, and therefore my power relationship to my opponent. This means that I can then use my centeredness to catch his power and channel it into the ground to strengthen my balance. From this position I can also break his balance through a neutralization technique and then move his body to a place where I can apply a joint lock or perform a throw.

In Second Level Training, we refine the power relationship so that when attacker and defender touch, center-to-center connection occurs. In Japanese this is called *ittai do*—mutual body. At that time of contact, our bodies automatically become one. That is the reason why practice and fighting strategies should always consist of first touch and neutralization at the same time, followed by a technique.

Question: How does spatial relationship affect timing?

Answer: With timing, and by this I mean the power relationship between defender and attacker, there are basically two ways to go—into or away from an attack. Our power relationship determines which of these two is the best direction to move. For example, if you are striking me with a punch, your target is my body. If I do not move, then you will be able to exert 100 percent of your power when you hit me. If I step forward before you punch, I am able to catch your movement and channel your power into the ground.

I can also move backward, or a little bit to one side, so that your power is not focused on its striking area. The places to move are almost unlimited, but the time is either before the punch, to stop your partner's power, or afterwards, to dissipate it.

Question: This timing or power relationship is easy to observe with a wrist grab. I grasp your wrist and push or pull and you have the time to feel it readily and relate to it. Is it the same with a strike, such as a punch to the face?

Answer: In the event of a strike, waiting to get hit is much worse than waiting to be grabbed—I don't recommend it. In real time it does not matter whether it is a strike or a grab. You are not going to offer your hand or wait for a strike; this kind of static training is for learning the power relationship. After you have mastered this static skill, you move to the next level of training —moving into or away to receive the attacker's power.

This movement—into or away—is part of timing and the power relationship, regardless of the attack. If it is a strike, you have to move to the point in the power relationship where you can channel your opponent's power into the ground to make your balance stronger and break his balance.

If you want to know how to distinguish between a strike and a grab, that is another level of training—learning your partner's intent.

Indeed, reading intent is the fourth level of training, learned through free sparring or free play. Making a centered, directed movement, so that you move as a unit to neutralize some of an attacker's power at the moment of contact, is something anyone can learn through observation and training. However, for whatever reason, creating timing and position is one of the most difficult techniques to master. While we can see what we have to do, it is often impossible to act expediently. Perhaps the reason is that, unlike a technique that one can plow through even as a beginner, timing can never be faked. Timing is an intuitive understanding of movement in space, like a blind pass in a basketball game or the interweaving of instruments in a Mozart symphony. It is a skill inherent in all of us that only practice can release.

CONCLUSION

When we started writing this book, the plan was to cover the subject of Aikido from basic training to reading an opponent's intent, including all of those heady epistimological and ontological issues associated with the martial arts which we knew lay beyond basic movement and technique. However, as we delved deeper into these principles, it was clear that a step lay between basic movement and those issues. That step became this book.

Our first chapters began laying the foundations of power in the martial arts. We noted that an attacker will eventually have to use his power to produce a positive result for him and a negative one for the defender. This led us to consider what is the best way to receive power. First, as laid out in Section One, we learned that it is possible to build a framework called centeredness that can become strengthened by receiving another person's power. The main components of centeredness were relaxation, proper body alignment, and ground connection.

The second aspect of receiving an opponent's power is to establish a center-to-center connection. We saw that finding or making a center-to-center connection can be a very natural process.

Somebody throws you an object; you catch it; before throwing it back, usually, you move it around in your hands feeling for the center. Once found, you instinctively know how best to hold it for the return throw. This is because every object has a natural center in relationship to its shape and mass. Locating it in an attacker is also a natural feeling, which is developed fully through Second Level Training. In fact, this sense must be trained to the point where it becomes automatic.

Let's return to our object, which we'll say is a basketball. We catch the ball, find its center, adjust it in relation to our center, and then throw it. If we don't do these steps, the throw is clumsy and weak. If we watch professional basketball players, we see that they have developed skills so that they can blend these steps into one smooth movement. Such fluidity is the goal of Second Level Training—to make a center-to-center connection at the moment of receiving power.

Based on this center-to-center power connection, in the second section of the book, we delineated three ways of neutralizing an opponent's power. We called these neutralization techniques grounding, uprooting, and spiraling. Either employed individually or in combination, these techniques severely diminish the amount of power an attacker can bring to bear on the defender.

Having studied the principles of power laid down in this book, we can learn how to move in relationship to an attack so that at the critical moment when an opponent fully commits, and says in effect, "Gotch ya!", he or she can be unbalanced by the defender without injury to either one. At the moment of first touch, the opponent's power is neutralized.

In the chapter, "Timing and Position," we explained a third step in the process; moving to the right place at the right time to take full advantage of the attacker's reduced power. Taking this principle further would involve not only moving to the right place at the right time, but doing so without knowing in advance what form the attack will take.

This would take us into a study of either free play or actual fighting, which we do not address in this book. However, *Center: The Power of Aikido* is based on responses to clear and specific attacks and the elements presented in this book will prove highly useful in all circumstances, from the practice hall to the boardroom.

For Second Level Training and Seminar opportunities contact:

Ron Meyer:

Phone: 303 444-1169 • e-mail: centrvid@ecentral.com

John Stone:

Phone: 608-231-3935 • e-mail: windfiend@aol.com

NOTES

1 These time frames may have to be adjusted for students' ages, strengths, and capabilities. In some cases, students will have to spend much longer periods of training within this progression.

2 A heavy medieval war club with a spiked or flanged metal head, used to crush armor.

3 See Chapter Five on Connection for a more complete explanation of the power relationship.

4 See Chapter Six on Grounding for a more detailed account of "breaking balance".

5 *Iriminage* literally means, "entering throw." In this Aikido technique, defender slips beside the opponent's attack into the dead space at his back. He then places his outside hand on the opponent's leading arm and the inside hand on the opponent's head. Pulling the opponent's head to his shoulder, defender then whirls in a 360 degree turn, taking the opponent's balance and throwing him to the ground.

6 See Chapter One on Power.

7 *Musubi* means joining together and unity. It can be used to explain the joining of opposites into a whole; or the unity of mind, spirit, and body; or linking the parts of the body together to form a cohesive unit that works like a single muscle.

8 See Chapter Four on Alignment and Chapter Five on Connection.

9 See Chapter Four on Alignment.

10 See Chapter One on Power.

11 *Kokyunage* literally means "breath throw" but the term is used to describe several categories of techniques involving throwing an

attacker forward or backward so that he or she falls to the ground away from the defender.

12 *Tenkan* means turning in a circle.

13 Mike Sigman, "Training Tip #5," *Internal Strength,* Issue #5, March 1994, p.15.

14 See Chapter Two on Centeredness.

15 *Shomenuchi* is a strike to the front of the head with the handor any weapon.

16 See Chapter Five on Connection.

17 See Chapter Two on Centeredness.

18 In *Daito Ryu Aikijitsu* it is also called *aikiage,* or breaking a partner's body balance.

19 *Ikkyo* is an Aikido technique where an opponent's strike to the face or grasp of the wrist is thrown back into him by driving his own elbow and wrist through his body and face toward the ground in a spiraling motion.

20 See Chapter Two on Centeredness.

21 See Chapter Eight on Spiraling.

22 See Chapter One on Power and Chapter Four on Alignment.

23 The Japanese term *musubi* can be used to describe the joining of two bodies from either a strike or a grab.

24 For purposes of simplification, the terms winding, twisting, and spinning will be considered components of spiraling and will not be used synonymously with the spiraling movement itself.

25 See *Internal Strength,* Issue #6, "Training Tips," May 1994, pp. 12–15, for a more complete explanation of the term "Reeling Silk."

26 Mike Sigman, "Training Tips," *Internal Strength,* Issue #6, May 1994, p.12.

BIBLIOGRAPHY

Crum, Thomas. *Journey to Center.* New York: Simon and Schuster, 1997.

Dobson, Terry and Miller, Victor. *Aikido in Everyday Life: Giving in to Get Your Way.* Berkeley: North Atlantic Books, 1978.

Dobson, Terry; Moss, Riki; and Watson, Jan E. *It's a Lot Like Dancing: An Aikido Journey.* Berkeley: Frog Ltd. 1992.

Fields, Rick. *The Awakened Warrior: Living with Courage, Compassion and Discipline.* New York: Putnam, 1994

Fields, Rick. *The Code of the Warrior.* New York: Harper Collins, 1993

Heckler, Richard Strozzi. *In Search of the Warrior Spirit.* Berkeley: North Atlantic Books, 1990.

Leonard, George. *Mastery: The Keys to Long-Term Success and Fulfillment.* New York: Penguin Books, 1991.

Leonard, George. *The Way of Aikido: Life Lessons from an American Sensei.* New York: Penguin, 1999.

Random, Michel. *The Martial Arts.* London: Octopus Books Ltd., 1978.

Stevens, John. *Abundant Peace: The Biography of Morihei Ueshiba. Founder of Aikido,* Boston: Shambhala, 1987.

Stone, John and Meyer, Ron. *Aikido in America.* Berkeley: Frog Ltd., 1995.

Warner, Judithn. *From Chaos to Center: A Training Guide in the Art of Centering.* New York. Aikiworks, Inc., 1999.